Mastering CLOUD COMPUTING

Concepts, Techniques, and Applications

Nikhilesh Mishra,
Author

Website
https://www.nikhileshmishra.com

Copyright Information

For permissions requests, write to the publisher at the address below:

Nikhilesh Mishra

Website: **https://www.nikhileshmishra.com**

Disclaimer: The information contained in this book is for educational and informational purposes only. It is not intended as a substitute for professional advice. The author and publisher disclaim any liability for the use of any information provided in this book.

Dedication

This book is lovingly dedicated to the cherished memory of my father, **Late Krishna Gopal Mishra**, and my mother**, Mrs. Vijay Kanti Mishra.** Their unwavering support, guidance, and love continue to inspire me.

Table of Contents

Author's Preface

Welcome to the captivating world of the knowledge we are about to explore! Within these pages, we invite you to embark on a journey that delves into the frontiers of information and understanding.

Charting the Path to Knowledge

Dive deep into the subjects we are about to explore as we unravel the intricate threads of innovation, creativity, and problem-solving. Whether you're a curious enthusiast, a seasoned professional, or an eager learner, this book serves as your gateway to gaining a deeper understanding.

Your Guiding Light

From the foundational principles of our chosen field to the advanced frontiers of its applications, we've meticulously crafted this book to be your trusted companion. Each chapter is an expedition, guided by expertise and filled with practical insights to empower you on your quest for knowledge.

What Awaits You

- **Illuminate the Origins:** Embark on a journey through the historical evolution of our chosen field, discovering key milestones that have paved the way for breakthroughs.

- **Demystify Complex Concepts:** Grasp the fundamental principles, navigate intricate concepts, and explore practical applications.
- **Mastery of the Craft:** Equip yourself with the skills and knowledge needed to excel in our chosen domain.

Your Journey Begins Here

As we embark on this enlightening journey together, remember that mastery is not just about knowledge but also the wisdom to apply it. Let each chapter be a stepping stone towards unlocking your potential, and let this book be your guide to becoming a true connoisseur of our chosen field.

So, turn the page, delve into the chapters, and immerse yourself in the world of knowledge. Let curiosity be your compass, and let the pursuit of understanding be your guide.

Begin your expedition now. Your quest for mastery awaits!

Sincerely,

Nikhilesh Mishra,

Author

CHAPTER 1

Introduction to Cloud Computing

Cloud computing is a transformative technology that has reshaped the landscape of modern IT infrastructure and services. In this chapter, we embark on a journey into the heart of cloud computing, where we will unravel its foundational concepts, evolution, and the pivotal role it plays in the digital age. Whether you're a seasoned professional looking to deepen your understanding or a newcomer seeking a solid foundation, this chapter serves as the gateway to a comprehensive exploration of cloud computing's intricacies. Join us as we demystify the cloud and discover the boundless opportunities it offers to individuals, organizations, and the ever-expanding digital ecosystem.

A. Definition and Evolution of Cloud Computing

In the early 2000s, the term "cloud computing" began to emerge as a novel paradigm in the world of technology. Initially, it was a nebulous concept, but over time, it has evolved into a fundamental and ubiquitous approach to delivering IT resources and services. In this chapter, we will delve into the definition and evolution of cloud computing, tracing its roots, understanding its core principles, and exploring how it has transformed the way we approach computing.

Defining Cloud Computing

At its essence, cloud computing is the delivery of computing services, including but not limited to servers, storage, databases, networking, software, analytics, and intelligence, over the internet ("the cloud") to offer faster innovation, flexible resources, and economies of scale. Instead of owning and managing physical hardware and software, users can access and use these resources on-demand, paying only for what they consume. The cloud can be thought of as a vast pool of shared resources, accessible from anywhere with an internet connection.

Key characteristics that define cloud computing include:

1. **On-Demand Self-Service:** Users can provision and manage resources as needed, without requiring human intervention from the service provider.

2. **Broad Network Access:** Cloud services are accessible over the internet and can be accessed by a variety of devices, including smartphones, laptops, and tablets.

3. **Resource Pooling:** Computing resources are pooled

together and shared among multiple users, ensuring efficient utilization and resource optimization.

4. **Rapid Elasticity:** Cloud resources can be scaled up or down quickly to accommodate changing workloads, ensuring flexibility and cost efficiency.

5. **Measured Service:** Cloud resources are metered, and users are billed based on their actual usage, promoting cost transparency.

The Evolution of Cloud Computing

The concept of cloud computing did not appear overnight but evolved over several decades, driven by advances in technology and changing business needs. Here's a brief overview of its evolution:

1. **Mainframes and Client-Server Computing (1950s-1980s):** The earliest computers were mainframes, massive machines that required users to access them via terminals. In the 1980s, client-server computing emerged, where smaller servers served the computing needs of multiple client machines.

2. **The Internet and Web 1.0 (1990s):** The growth of the internet and the World Wide Web laid the foundation for remote data access and the idea of "online" services. This era saw the birth of early web-based applications and services.

3. **Utility and Grid Computing (1990s-2000s):** Concepts like utility computing and grid computing introduced the idea of sharing computing resources on a broader scale, but these models were often complex and primarily used in research and academia.

4. **Virtualization (2000s):** Virtualization technologies, especially server virtualization, played a pivotal role in cloud computing's development. Virtual machines enabled better resource utilization and isolation, setting the stage for cloud services.

5. **The Emergence of Cloud Providers (2000s):** Companies like Amazon Web Services (AWS), Google Cloud, and Microsoft Azure began offering cloud services, making it easier for businesses to access and utilize remote computing resources.

6. **Proliferation of Cloud Services (2010s):** Cloud services evolved beyond infrastructure (IaaS) to include platforms (PaaS) and software applications (SaaS). This decade also witnessed the rise of serverless computing, containerization, and microservices.

7. **Edge Computing and Beyond (2020s and beyond):** The cloud continues to evolve with trends like edge computing, quantum computing integration, and increased focus on ethics and sustainability in cloud technology.

Today, cloud computing is not just a technology; it's a fundamental enabler of innovation and digital transformation across industries. Its evolution continues to shape the way we work, connect, and solve complex problems in our increasingly digital world. In the subsequent chapters of this book, we will explore the various facets of cloud computing in greater detail, from its service models and deployment options to security, cost management, and emerging trends.

B. Key Concepts in Cloud Computing: Virtualization, Scalability, and Elasticity

To truly grasp the essence of cloud computing, one must delve into the key concepts that underpin its functionality and appeal. Among these foundational concepts are virtualization, scalability, and elasticity, each playing a crucial role in the cloud's ability to deliver flexible, efficient, and cost-effective computing solutions. In this section, we will explore these concepts in depth, shedding light on their significance within the cloud computing landscape.

1. Virtualization:

Virtualization is a cornerstone of cloud computing, allowing for the efficient utilization of physical hardware resources by creating virtual instances of computing environments. Here's a closer look at virtualization:

a. Hardware Abstraction: Virtualization abstracts physical hardware, such as servers, storage, and networking, into software-defined components. This abstraction decouples the virtual resources from the underlying physical infrastructure, enabling greater flexibility.

b. Virtual Machines (VMs): VMs are virtualized instances of a physical computer, complete with an operating system and applications. They enable multiple workloads to run on a single physical server, maximizing resource utilization.

c. Hypervisors: Hypervisors are software or firmware that manages VMs on a physical server. They allocate resources, isolate VMs, and facilitate efficient resource sharing.

d. Benefits: Virtualization provides benefits like hardware consolidation, resource isolation, and the ability to run diverse workloads on a single infrastructure. It forms the foundation for cloud infrastructure, allowing for the rapid provisioning of VMs in response to demand.

2. Scalability:

Scalability in cloud computing refers to the system's ability to handle varying workloads by adding or removing resources seamlessly. There are two types of scalability:

a. Vertical Scalability (Scaling Up): This involves increasing the resources (e.g., CPU, RAM) of an individual component within a system, such as upgrading a server with more memory or processing power. While vertical scalability improves the performance of a single component, it has limits and can be costly.

b. Horizontal Scalability (Scaling Out): Horizontal scalability involves adding more identical components to the system, typically in a distributed fashion. For example, adding more web servers to a cluster. This approach provides better overall system scalability, as it can accommodate increased load by adding more instances.

c. Benefits: Scalability ensures that cloud-based applications and services can handle fluctuations in demand without performance degradation. It aligns resource usage and costs with actual usage patterns, optimizing efficiency.

3. Elasticity:

Elasticity is an extension of scalability but adds the automated and dynamic nature of resource provisioning to meet changing demands. Key aspects of elasticity include:

a. Auto-Scaling: Cloud platforms allow users to configure auto-scaling rules based on predefined metrics (e.g., CPU utilization, network traffic). When traffic spikes or decreases, the system automatically adds or removes resources to maintain performance and cost-efficiency.

b. Pay-as-You-Go: Elasticity aligns with the cloud's pay-as-you-go model, where users only pay for the resources they consume. When demand drops, resources are automatically deprovisioned, reducing costs.

c. Cloud Orchestration: Tools and services for cloud orchestration, like Kubernetes, facilitate the automation of resource scaling and management based on predefined policies.

d. Benefits: Elasticity ensures that resources are provisioned and deprovisioned dynamically, eliminating the need for manual intervention and optimizing cost efficiency.

In summary, virtualization, scalability, and elasticity are three critical concepts that define the flexibility and efficiency of cloud computing. Virtualization abstracts and optimizes hardware resources, scalability allows for growth or reduction of resources as needed, and elasticity ensures that these changes happen automatically to meet real-time demands. Understanding and effectively utilizing these concepts are essential for harnessing the full potential of cloud computing, whether for hosting applications, processing data, or delivering services to users around the globe.

C. Cloud Service Models: IaaS, PaaS, and SaaS

Cloud computing offers a range of service models that cater to different user needs and requirements. These models, often referred to as IaaS (Infrastructure as a Service), PaaS (Platform as a Service), and SaaS (Software as a Service), represent varying levels of abstraction and management responsibilities. In this in-depth exploration, we will dissect these cloud service models to help you understand their distinct characteristics, use cases, and advantages.

1. Infrastructure as a Service (IaaS):

Definition: IaaS is the foundational layer of cloud computing. It provides virtualized computing resources over the internet, allowing users to rent and manage infrastructure components like virtual machines, storage, and networking.

Key Characteristics:

- **Resource Flexibility:** IaaS offers a flexible, on-demand approach to computing resources. Users can provision and configure virtual machines, storage, and networking according to their specific requirements.

- **User Management:** Users are responsible for managing the operating system, applications, and data hosted on the virtual machines. This grants them greater control over the infrastructure.

- **Scalability:** IaaS platforms allow users to scale

resources up or down based on demand. This makes it suitable for a wide range of use cases, from hosting web applications to running development and testing environments.

Use Cases:

- **Development and Testing:** IaaS is commonly used for development and testing environments, where teams can quickly provision resources, test software, and then release them when no longer needed.

- **Web Hosting:** Many websites and web applications are hosted on IaaS platforms due to their scalability and control over server configurations.

Advantages:

- **Control:** Users have full control over the infrastructure, including the operating system and software stack.

- **Flexibility:** Resources can be customized to suit specific requirements.

2. Platform as a Service (PaaS):

Definition: PaaS is a cloud service model that provides a platform and environment for developers to build, deploy, and manage applications. It abstracts the underlying infrastructure, focusing on application development and deployment.

Key Characteristics:

- **Development Focus:** PaaS platforms provide tools, development frameworks, and runtime environments for building and deploying applications. Developers can concentrate on writing code without concerning themselves with underlying infrastructure details.

- **Managed Services:** PaaS offerings often include managed services like databases, messaging systems, and development tools, simplifying application development.

- **Scalability:** PaaS platforms handle automatic scaling, making it easy to accommodate changes in application usage.

Use Cases:

- **Web Application Development:** PaaS is ideal for developing web applications, APIs, and microservices. Popular platforms like Heroku and Google App Engine fall into this category.

- **Mobile App Development:** PaaS can be used to create and deploy mobile applications.

Advantages:

- **Simplified Development:** Developers can focus on writing code rather than managing infrastructure.

- **Managed Services:** Built-in services reduce the operational burden.

3. Software as a Service (SaaS):

Definition: SaaS is the highest level of abstraction in cloud computing. It delivers software applications over the internet on a subscription basis, eliminating the need for users to install, maintain, or manage the software locally.

Key Characteristics:

- **Ready-to-Use:** SaaS applications are fully functional and accessible via web browsers or dedicated clients. Users simply log in and use the software without worrying about installation or maintenance.

- **Automatic Updates:** SaaS providers manage software updates, ensuring users always have access to the latest features and security patches.

- **Multi-Tenancy:** SaaS applications are often multi-tenant, serving multiple customers from a shared infrastructure.

Use Cases:

- **Email and Collaboration Tools:** Examples include Gmail, Microsoft Office 365, and Slack.

- **Customer Relationship Management (CRM):** Salesforce is a popular SaaS CRM platform.

Advantages:

- **Ease of Use:** SaaS applications are user-friendly and accessible from anywhere with an internet connection.

- **Automatic Updates:** Users benefit from continuous improvements and security updates without manual intervention.

Choosing the Right Service Model:

Selecting the appropriate service model depends on your specific needs, technical expertise, and desired level of control. Organizations often use a combination of these models to address various aspects of their IT infrastructure and application development lifecycle. Understanding the distinctions among IaaS, PaaS, and SaaS is essential for making informed decisions about cloud adoption and optimizing resource utilization in the cloud environment.

D. Deployment Models in Cloud Computing: Public, Private, Hybrid, and Multi-Cloud

Cloud computing deployment models define how and where cloud resources are hosted, managed, and accessed. These models offer varying degrees of control, security, and flexibility. In this comprehensive exploration, we will delve into the four main deployment models: Public Cloud, Private Cloud, Hybrid Cloud, and Multi-Cloud, discussing their characteristics, use cases, benefits, and considerations.

1. Public Cloud:

Definition: The public cloud is a deployment model in which cloud services and infrastructure are owned, operated, and provided by third-party cloud service providers. These services are made available to the public on a pay-as-you-go basis.

Key Characteristics:

- **Shared Infrastructure:** Public cloud resources are shared among multiple customers, resulting in cost efficiencies due to economies of scale.

- **Accessibility:** Services are accessible over the internet, making them readily available to users from anywhere with an internet connection.

- **Scalability:** Public clouds offer automatic scalability, allowing users to increase or decrease resources as needed.

Use Cases:

- **Web Hosting:** Hosting websites and web applications is a common use case for the public cloud due to its scalability and cost-effectiveness.

- **Development and Testing:** Developers can provision temporary resources for development and testing without the need for on-premises infrastructure.

Advantages:

- **Cost-Efficiency:** Pay-as-you-go pricing means users only pay for the resources they consume.

- **Scalability:** Resources can be scaled up or down based on demand.

Considerations:

- **Security and Compliance:** Public cloud users must address security and compliance concerns, especially when handling sensitive data.

2. Private Cloud:

Definition: Private cloud is a deployment model that involves dedicated cloud infrastructure provisioned for a single organization or entity. It can be hosted on-premises or by a third-party provider.

Key Characteristics:

- **Isolation:** Private clouds offer a higher level of

isolation and control compared to public clouds. Resources are not shared with other organizations.

- **Customization:** Organizations have the flexibility to customize the cloud environment to meet their specific requirements.

Use Cases:

- **Data Security and Compliance:** Industries with strict data security and compliance requirements, such as finance and healthcare, often opt for private clouds.

- **Mission-Critical Workloads:** Private clouds are suitable for running mission-critical applications where reliability and performance are paramount.

Advantages:

- **Control:** Organizations have full control over the private cloud infrastructure.

- **Security:** Private clouds offer enhanced security and data isolation.

Considerations:

- **Cost:** Private clouds can be more expensive to set up and maintain compared to public cloud solutions.

3. Hybrid Cloud:

Definition: The hybrid cloud is a deployment model that combines elements of both public and private clouds. It allows data and applications to be shared between them.

Key Characteristics:

- **Integration:** Hybrid clouds are designed to facilitate seamless data and workload movement between public and private cloud environments.

- **Flexibility:** Organizations can leverage the scalability and cost-efficiency of the public cloud while maintaining sensitive data and critical workloads in a private cloud.

Use Cases:

- **Bursting:** Organizations can use public cloud resources to handle spikes in demand while running their core workloads in a private cloud.

- **Data Backup and Disaster Recovery:** Data can be replicated and backed up in a public cloud for redundancy and disaster recovery purposes.

Advantages:

- **Flexibility:** Hybrid clouds offer the flexibility to balance cost, performance, and security requirements.

- **Scalability:** Organizations can scale resources dynamically as needed.

Considerations:

- **Complexity:** Managing a hybrid cloud environment can be more complex than a single deployment model.

4. Multi-Cloud:

Definition: Multi-cloud is a deployment strategy that involves using services from multiple cloud providers, either simultaneously or interchangeably, to meet specific needs.

Key Characteristics:

- **Diverse Services:** Organizations select the best-fit cloud providers for specific services or applications, optimizing costs and performance.

- **Vendor Independence:** Multi-cloud environments reduce vendor lock-in, as organizations are not reliant on a single provider.

Use Cases:

- **Best-of-Breed Services:** Organizations can choose the best services from different providers, such as leveraging AWS for machine learning and Azure for data analytics.

- **Risk Mitigation:** Multi-cloud strategies can help mitigate risks associated with service outages or disruptions from a single provider.

Advantages:

- **Flexibility:** Multi-cloud provides the flexibility to adapt to changing business needs and technology trends.

- **Risk Mitigation:** Organizations can reduce the impact of service disruptions by diversifying their cloud providers.

Considerations:

- **Management:** Managing multiple cloud providers requires robust governance and management practices to ensure efficiency and cost control.

In conclusion, the choice of a cloud deployment model depends on an organization's specific needs, including data sensitivity, compliance requirements, and resource scalability. Many organizations adopt a hybrid or multi-cloud approach to leverage the strengths of various deployment models and providers while managing associated complexities effectively. Understanding these deployment models is essential for crafting a cloud strategy that aligns with an organization's goals and requirements.

E. Benefits and Challenges of Cloud Computing

Cloud computing has transformed the way businesses and individuals access and utilize IT resources. Its adoption has brought about numerous benefits, but it also presents its share of challenges. In this comprehensive analysis, we will delve into the key advantages and potential drawbacks of cloud computing.

Benefits of Cloud Computing:

1. **Cost Efficiency:**

- **Pay-as-You-Go:** Cloud services operate on a subscription or pay-as-you-go model, allowing organizations to pay only for the resources they use. This eliminates the need for large upfront investments in hardware and reduces ongoing operational costs.

- **Resource Optimization:** Cloud providers maximize resource utilization through virtualization, resulting in cost savings.

- **Economies of Scale:** Cloud providers benefit from economies of scale, allowing them to offer cost-effective services to customers.

2. **Scalability and Flexibility:**

- **Elasticity:** Cloud resources can be scaled up or down

based on demand, ensuring that organizations can handle varying workloads efficiently.

- **Global Reach:** Cloud providers offer data centers and services worldwide, enabling businesses to expand their operations globally without building physical infrastructure.

3. **Accessibility and Collaboration:**

- **Remote Access:** Cloud services are accessible from anywhere with an internet connection, promoting remote work and collaboration.

- **Real-Time Collaboration:** Cloud-based collaboration tools facilitate real-time document editing and sharing among teams.

4. **Reliability and Redundancy:**

- **High Availability:** Cloud providers offer high availability and uptime guarantees, reducing the risk of service disruptions.

- **Data Redundancy:** Cloud providers replicate data across multiple data centers, safeguarding against data loss due to hardware failures.

5. **Security:**

- **Security Expertise:** Cloud providers invest heavily in

security measures, often employing dedicated security teams and technologies.

- **Compliance:** Many cloud providers offer compliance certifications, helping organizations meet regulatory requirements.

6. **Automatic Updates and Maintenance:**

- **Effortless Maintenance:** Cloud providers handle software updates, patches, and maintenance tasks, reducing the operational burden on users.

Challenges of Cloud Computing:

1. **Security Concerns:**

- **Data Privacy:** Storing data on third-party servers can raise concerns about data privacy and confidentiality.

- **Data Breaches:** High-profile data breaches have occurred, highlighting the importance of robust security measures and user diligence.

2. **Downtime and Service Outages:**

- **Dependency on Providers:** Organizations rely on cloud providers for service availability, making them vulnerable to provider outages.

- **Internet Dependency:** Access to cloud services requires a stable internet connection, which may not be available everywhere.

3. **Data Transfer and Bandwidth Costs:**

- **Data Transfer Fees:** Moving large volumes of data in and out of the cloud can incur additional costs, impacting budget considerations.

- **Bandwidth Limitations:** Limited bandwidth can affect the speed and efficiency of data transfers.

4. **Vendor Lock-In:**

- **Compatibility Issues:** Transitioning away from one cloud provider to another can be complex and costly due to compatibility and data migration challenges.

- **Integration Challenges:** Organizations may face difficulties integrating cloud services with their existing on-premises systems.

5. **Compliance and Legal Issues:**

- **Jurisdictional Concerns:** Data stored in the cloud may be subject to different legal jurisdictions, complicating compliance efforts.

- **Data Ownership:** Clarifying data ownership and

responsibility in case of legal disputes can be challenging.

6. **Performance Variability:**

- **Shared Resources:** In multi-tenant environments, performance may be affected by neighboring users sharing the same physical infrastructure.

- **Latency:** Network latency can impact the responsiveness of cloud-based applications, particularly for latency-sensitive workloads.

7. **Data Loss and Recovery:**

- **Data Loss Risks:** While cloud providers employ robust data redundancy measures, data loss can still occur due to various factors, including human error and cyberattacks.

- **Data Recovery Complexity:** Restoring data in the event of a failure may require careful planning and coordination with the provider.

In conclusion, cloud computing offers significant advantages, including cost savings, scalability, and accessibility. However, organizations must carefully consider and mitigate the associated challenges, such as security concerns, data transfer costs, and vendor lock-in. A well-planned cloud strategy, including risk assessment and compliance measures, is essential for reaping the benefits of cloud computing while minimizing potential pitfalls.

CHAPTER 2

Cloud Infrastructure

In the digital age, where data flows ceaselessly and the demands on computing power grow exponentially, the foundation upon which our virtual world is built becomes paramount. Cloud infrastructure stands as the bedrock of this new era, offering the agility, scalability, and reliability necessary to support the ever-evolving needs of businesses and individuals alike. In this exploration, we embark on a journey through the intricate realms of cloud infrastructure, unraveling its core components, technologies, and the critical role it plays in reshaping our digital landscape. Join us as we delve into the architecture and mechanics that power the cloud, the unseen force behind our interconnected world.

A. Data Centers and Server Farms: The Cornerstones of Cloud Infrastructure

In the realm of cloud computing, data centers and server farms are the unsung heroes, providing the physical and virtual foundations upon which the digital world thrives. These interconnected hubs of computational power, storage, and networking form the backbone of cloud infrastructure. In this comprehensive exploration, we will delve into the intricacies of data centers and server farms, uncovering their vital roles, design considerations, and the evolving technologies that drive their operation.

Data Centers: The Nerve Centers of the Cloud

Definition: A data center is a centralized facility or building that houses computing hardware, including servers, storage devices, networking equipment, and other critical components. Its primary purpose is to store, manage, and process data, applications, and services for organizations or cloud service providers.

Key Components and Considerations:

1. **Servers:** Data centers are populated with racks of servers, each containing multiple CPUs and memory modules. These servers handle various tasks, from hosting websites to running applications.

2. **Networking Infrastructure:** High-speed, redundant networking equipment ensures data can flow seamlessly within the data center and to external networks. This includes switches, routers, and load balancers.

3. **Storage Systems:** Data centers feature an array of storage solutions, including traditional hard disk drives (HDDs)

and solid-state drives (SSDs) for data storage and retrieval.

4. **Redundancy and Backup:** Data centers employ redundancy at multiple levels, from power supplies and cooling systems to networking and storage, to minimize downtime and data loss.

5. **Cooling and Climate Control:** Maintaining optimal temperature and humidity levels is crucial to prevent overheating and hardware failure. Data centers use advanced cooling systems to manage the environment.

6. **Physical Security:** Data centers are typically equipped with robust physical security measures, including access control, surveillance, and security personnel, to protect against unauthorized access.

7. **Scalability:** Data centers are designed to be scalable, allowing for the addition of hardware as computing needs grow.

Server Farms: The Powerhouses of Compute

Definition: Server farms, also known as server clusters or server arrays, are groups of interconnected servers that work collectively to deliver high-performance computing and redundancy. These farms are often found within data centers and are designed for specific purposes, such as web hosting, content delivery, or database management.

Key Characteristics and Uses:

1. **Load Balancing:** Server farms employ load balancers to distribute incoming requests or network traffic evenly across multiple servers. This ensures efficient resource utilization and improved response times.

2. **High Availability:** Redundant server configurations and failover mechanisms are common in server farms to maintain service availability even in the event of hardware failures.

3. **Specialized Clusters:** Some server farms are tailored for specific tasks, such as rendering graphics, performing scientific simulations, or supporting virtualization platforms.

4. **Content Delivery:** Content delivery networks (CDNs) use server farms strategically positioned around the globe to deliver web content, streaming media, and large files with low latency.

The Evolution of Data Centers and Server Farms:

Over the years, data centers and server farms have undergone significant transformations driven by advances in technology and changing business needs:

- **Virtualization:** Server virtualization technologies, such as VMware and Hyper-V, have enabled the consolidation of multiple virtual machines on a single physical server, optimizing resource utilization.

- **Modular Design:** Data centers now often employ modular design principles, allowing for the rapid deployment of new capacity as needed.

- **Cloud Integration:** Many organizations integrate their on-premises data centers with public or private cloud services, creating hybrid cloud environments that offer flexibility and scalability.

- **Edge Computing:** With the rise of IoT and the need for real-time processing, edge data centers and server farms are emerging at the network's edge to reduce latency and improve responsiveness.

In conclusion, data centers and server farms are the backbone of modern cloud infrastructure, providing the physical and computational resources necessary to power the digital world. Their evolution continues to shape the way businesses and individuals access and utilize cloud-based services, enabling a connected, data-driven society. Understanding their design principles and evolving technologies is essential for organizations seeking to leverage cloud computing effectively.

B. Virtualization Technologies: Unleashing the Power of Cloud Computing

Virtualization technologies are the driving force behind the agility, efficiency, and cost savings that have made cloud computing a game-changer in the world of IT. These technologies abstract physical hardware, allowing multiple virtualized instances to run on a single physical server, optimizing resource utilization and enhancing flexibility. In this in-depth exploration, we will dive into the world of virtualization, exploring its types, benefits, and the pivotal role it plays in the modern cloud infrastructure.

Types of Virtualization:

1. **Server Virtualization:**

- **Definition:** Server virtualization involves creating multiple virtual machines (VMs) on a single physical server, each running its own operating system and applications.

- **Benefits:** Server virtualization maximizes hardware utilization, enables workload isolation, and simplifies resource provisioning.

2. **Storage Virtualization:**

- **Definition:** Storage virtualization abstracts physical storage devices and combines them into a single pool of storage resources. It allows for more efficient allocation and management of storage capacity.

- **Benefits:** Storage virtualization simplifies storage management, improves data availability, and enhances scalability.

3. **Network Virtualization:**

- **Definition:** Network virtualization abstracts network resources, enabling the creation of virtual networks that operate independently of the physical network infrastructure. Technologies like VLANs and SDN (Software-Defined Networking) play a crucial role in network virtualization.

- **Benefits:** Network virtualization enhances network agility, simplifies network provisioning, and improves security through network segmentation.

Key Benefits of Virtualization Technologies:

1. **Resource Optimization:**

- Virtualization allows for the efficient use of physical resources by consolidating multiple workloads onto a single server, reducing hardware and operational costs.

2. **Isolation and Security:**

- Virtual machines and virtual networks can be isolated from one another, enhancing security by preventing interference between workloads.

3. **Flexibility and Scalability:**

- Virtualization enables the dynamic allocation and reallocation of resources, making it easier to scale up or down based on demand.

4. **Hardware Independence:**

- Virtualization abstracts hardware, allowing virtualized workloads to run on different physical servers without modification.

5. **Disaster Recovery and Redundancy:**

- Virtualization technologies facilitate data backup, replication, and disaster recovery solutions, ensuring data and applications remain available even in the event of hardware failures.

6. **Energy Efficiency:**

- Server virtualization can reduce energy consumption by consolidating workloads onto fewer physical servers.

Hypervisors: The Foundation of Virtualization:

At the core of server virtualization lies the hypervisor, a specialized software or firmware layer responsible for managing and allocating physical resources to virtual machines. There are two main types of hypervisors:

1. **Type 1 Hypervisor (Bare-Metal):**

- Type 1 hypervisors run directly on the physical hardware without the need for a host operating system. Examples include VMware vSphere/ESXi and Microsoft Hyper-V.

- They offer better performance and security but require more specialized management.

2. **Type 2 Hypervisor (Hosted):**

- Type 2 hypervisors run on top of an existing host operating system. Examples include VMware Workstation and Oracle VirtualBox.

- They are easier to set up but introduce some performance overhead.

Challenges and Considerations:

While virtualization brings numerous benefits, it also poses some challenges:

1. **Resource Overcommitment:** Overcommitting resources can lead to performance degradation if not managed properly.

2. **Management Complexity:** Managing a virtualized environment can be complex, especially in large-scale deployments.

3. **Security Concerns:** Vulnerabilities in hypervisors or misconfigurations can pose security risks.

4. **Licensing Costs:** Some virtualization solutions have licensing costs, which can impact the overall cost savings.

In conclusion, virtualization technologies are the linchpin of modern cloud computing, enabling organizations to optimize resources, enhance flexibility, and reduce costs. As the foundation upon which cloud services are built, understanding the nuances of virtualization is essential for harnessing the full potential of the cloud and delivering agile, scalable, and cost-effective IT solutions.

C. Storage Systems in Cloud Computing: Block, Object, and File Storage

In the world of cloud computing, efficient and scalable storage solutions are paramount. Different storage systems cater to various use cases and requirements, offering a diverse array of functionalities and advantages. In this in-depth exploration, we will delve into three fundamental storage systems: Block Storage, Object Storage, and File Storage, dissecting their characteristics, use cases, and how they contribute to the architecture of modern cloud environments.

1. Block Storage:

Definition: Block storage is a type of storage system that manages data in fixed-sized blocks or chunks. Each block is treated as an independent storage unit and can be addressed individually.

Characteristics:

- **Low-Level Access:** Block storage provides the lowest-level access to data, making it ideal for situations where fine-grained control is necessary.

- **Performance:** Block storage systems offer high-performance capabilities and are suitable for applications that require low latency and high I/O operations, such as databases.

Use Cases:

- **Database Storage:** Block storage is commonly used to store databases due to its low latency and predictable performance.

- **Virtual Machine Storage:** It is also used for hosting virtual machine disks in infrastructure-as-a-service (IaaS) environments.

Advantages:

- **Performance:** Block storage systems offer excellent performance for applications requiring high-speed data access.

- **Data Consistency:** They ensure data consistency and integrity, making them suitable for critical applications.

2. Object Storage:

Definition: Object storage is a storage system that manages data as objects, where each object contains the data, metadata, and a unique identifier. Objects are stored in a flat namespace and can be organized hierarchically.

Characteristics:

- **Scalability:** Object storage systems are highly scalable and can store vast amounts of unstructured data.

- **Metadata:** They store metadata alongside data, which facilitates data categorization and retrieval.

Use Cases:

- **Backup and Archive:** Object storage is well-suited for backup and long-term data retention, as it can accommodate massive datasets.

- **Content Delivery:** Content delivery networks (CDNs)

often use object storage to distribute large files, videos, and images efficiently.

Advantages:

- **Scalability:** Object storage systems can handle petabytes of data or more, making them ideal for storing large datasets.

- **Durability:** They are designed for high data durability, ensuring data remains intact even in the face of hardware failures.

3. File Storage:

Definition: File storage is a storage system that manages data in hierarchical directories and files, similar to how data is organized on a traditional file system.

Characteristics:

- **Hierarchical Structure:** File storage systems use a hierarchical directory structure for organizing data.

- **Network Access:** They allow multiple users or systems to access files over a network, making them suitable for shared file storage.

Use Cases:

- **User Home Directories:** File storage is commonly

used for providing users with personal file storage areas.

- **Network Shares:** It is used for shared network drives and file sharing in organizations.

Advantages:

- **Familiarity:** Users and applications are familiar with file-based access patterns, making file storage a straightforward choice for many scenarios.

- **Collaboration:** File storage systems are conducive to collaboration as multiple users can access and modify files simultaneously.

Considerations:

- **Concurrency:** Handling concurrent access by multiple users can be a challenge and may require file locking mechanisms to prevent data conflicts.

- **Performance:** While file storage is suitable for many use cases, it may not offer the same level of performance as block storage for certain high-throughput applications.

In conclusion, storage systems are integral to cloud computing, and each type serves distinct purposes. Block storage provides low-level access and high performance, object storage excels at scalability and data durability, and file storage offers familiarity and collaboration features. Choosing the right storage system depends on the specific use case and requirements, and many cloud providers offer a combination of these storage options to meet diverse needs within a cloud environment.

D. Networking in the Cloud: Connecting the Digital World

Networking is the circulatory system of the cloud, enabling the flow of data and services to and from cloud resources. It forms the foundation upon which modern cloud computing is built, facilitating communication, scalability, security, and accessibility. In this comprehensive exploration, we will delve into the intricate world of networking in the cloud, dissecting its components, key technologies, and the pivotal role it plays in shaping the digital landscape.

Key Components of Networking in the Cloud:

1. **Virtual Private Cloud (VPC):**

- **Definition:** A Virtual Private Cloud (VPC) is a logically isolated network within a public cloud infrastructure, such as AWS or Azure. It allows users to define their own private IP address space, create subnets, and manage network traffic.

- **Benefits:** VPCs provide network isolation and segmentation, allowing organizations to control access and security within their cloud environment.

2. **Content Delivery Networks (CDNs):**

- **Definition:** CDNs are distributed networks of servers strategically placed at multiple data centers worldwide. They cache and deliver web content, including images, videos, and static files, to users from a location nearest to them, reducing latency and improving content delivery speed.

- **Benefits:** CDNs enhance the performance and availability of web applications by reducing server load and speeding up content delivery.

3. **Cloud Networking Protocols:**

- Cloud environments rely on standard networking protocols like TCP/IP, UDP, and BGP (Border Gateway Protocol) for communication between cloud resources, data centers, and the broader internet.

4. **Load Balancers:**

- **Definition:** Load balancers distribute incoming network traffic across multiple servers or resources to ensure even resource utilization and prevent overloading of specific servers.

- **Benefits:** Load balancers enhance application availability, scalability, and fault tolerance by evenly distributing traffic and redirecting it away from unhealthy servers.

5. **Firewalls and Network Security Groups:**

- Firewalls and network security groups are used to control inbound and outbound network traffic to and from cloud resources. They enforce security policies and restrict unauthorized access.

Key Networking Technologies in Cloud Computing:

1. **Software-Defined Networking (SDN):**

- **Definition:** SDN is a networking paradigm that separates the control plane from the data plane in network devices, enabling centralized network management and dynamic network configuration.

- **Benefits:** SDN simplifies network provisioning, improves agility, and allows for dynamic traffic routing and load balancing.

2. **Virtual Private Network (VPN):**

- **Definition:** VPNs establish secure, encrypted connections between on-premises networks and cloud environments, allowing for secure data transfer and remote access.

- **Use Cases:** VPNs are commonly used for connecting branch offices, remote workers, and external partners to cloud resources.

3. **Direct Connect/ExpressRoute:**

- **Definition:** Direct Connect (AWS) and ExpressRoute (Azure) are dedicated network connections that provide private and dedicated connectivity between on-premises data centers and cloud providers, bypassing the public internet.

- **Benefits:** These services offer low-latency, high-bandwidth connections, ensuring reliable and secure communication between on-premises and cloud resources.

Security Considerations in Cloud Networking:

1. **Network Security Groups (NSGs):** NSGs allow organizations to control inbound and outbound traffic to and from Azure resources. They act as firewall rules and help enforce network security policies.

2. **Virtual Private Cloud Isolation:** Properly configuring VPCs or similar constructs in other cloud providers is crucial for isolating resources and controlling network traffic.

3. **DDoS Mitigation:** Cloud providers often offer DDoS (Distributed Denial of Service) protection services to safeguard against network attacks.

4. **Encryption:** Encrypting data in transit and at rest is

essential for maintaining data security within a cloud network.

5. **Identity and Access Management (IAM):** Properly configuring IAM policies ensures that only authorized users and services can access network resources.

In conclusion, networking in the cloud is a complex but essential aspect of modern computing. It underpins the connectivity, performance, and security of cloud environments, enabling organizations to leverage cloud resources efficiently while ensuring data integrity and accessibility. Understanding the principles of cloud networking is paramount for designing and maintaining reliable and secure cloud solutions.

E. Cloud Hardware and Software: The Engine and Control Panel of Cloud Computing

Cloud computing is often depicted as a nebulous concept, but it relies heavily on tangible infrastructure and software systems. In this comprehensive exploration, we will delve into the realms of cloud hardware and software, unraveling the technology that powers the cloud and the orchestration tools that manage it.

Cloud Hardware: The Physical Backbone

Cloud hardware encompasses the tangible physical components that make up the cloud infrastructure. This hardware includes servers, storage devices, networking equipment, and specialized components designed to operate efficiently and at scale within data centers. Here are the key elements of cloud hardware:

1. **Servers:** Servers form the core of cloud hardware. They are high-performance computers designed to run applications, store data, and process requests. Within cloud data centers, servers are often organized into racks and clusters.

2. **Storage Devices:** Cloud providers use various types of storage devices, including hard disk drives (HDDs), solid-state drives (SSDs), and specialized storage arrays to store data. Redundancy and fault tolerance are built into storage systems to ensure data durability.

3. **Networking Equipment:** High-speed networking equipment, such as switches, routers, load balancers, and firewalls, connect servers and storage devices, allowing data to flow efficiently within the cloud infrastructure and between data centers.

4. **Data Centers:** Data centers are the physical facilities where cloud hardware is housed. These centers are designed to provide a controlled environment with regulated temperature, humidity, and security measures to ensure reliable operation.

5. **Specialized Hardware:** Some cloud providers deploy specialized hardware, such as GPUs (Graphics Processing Units)

or TPUs (Tensor Processing Units), for specific tasks like machine learning and AI workloads.

6. **Power and Cooling Systems:** Ensuring continuous power supply and efficient cooling is crucial to maintain the operational integrity of cloud hardware. Data centers often employ backup power sources and advanced cooling mechanisms.

Cloud Software: The Control and Management Layer

While cloud hardware forms the foundation, cloud software serves as the control panel, managing the provisioning, scaling, and orchestration of cloud resources. Here are the key elements of cloud software:

1. **Hypervisors:** Hypervisors are essential software components that enable server virtualization. They allow multiple virtual machines (VMs) to run on a single physical server, optimizing resource utilization.

2. **Orchestration and Management Tools:** Cloud providers use orchestration and management software to automate resource provisioning, configuration, scaling, and monitoring. Examples include Amazon CloudFormation and Azure Resource Manager.

3. **Container Orchestration:** Container orchestration platforms like Kubernetes manage the deployment, scaling, and

operation of containerized applications, making it easier to build and manage microservices-based applications.

4. **Operating Systems:** Cloud servers run specialized operating systems optimized for cloud environments. These operating systems often include features for automatic updates, security management, and resource allocation.

5. **Cloud Management Platforms:** These platforms provide centralized control and visibility into cloud resources, enabling organizations to manage and optimize their cloud infrastructure efficiently.

6. **Security and Compliance Tools:** Cloud software includes security and compliance solutions to protect cloud resources and ensure compliance with regulations like GDPR and HIPAA.

7. **Monitoring and Logging Tools:** Cloud providers offer monitoring and logging tools to track the performance, availability, and security of cloud resources. Examples include AWS CloudWatch and Azure Monitor.

8. **Database and Middleware Services:** Cloud software includes managed database services and middleware platforms that simplify the deployment and management of databases and application components.

The Role of Virtualization in Cloud Hardware and Software:

Virtualization technologies, including hypervisors and containerization, play a crucial role in cloud computing. They enable the efficient sharing and allocation of hardware resources among multiple users and workloads, enhancing flexibility and cost-effectiveness.

Challenges in Cloud Hardware and Software:

1. **Scalability:** Cloud providers must continuously scale their hardware and software to meet increasing demand while maintaining performance and reliability.

2. **Security:** Protecting cloud infrastructure from security threats, including data breaches and cyberattacks, is a constant challenge.

3. **Cost Management:** Optimizing costs while delivering performance and scalability can be complex, requiring careful resource planning and allocation.

4. **Complexity:** Managing the complexity of large-scale cloud infrastructure and software systems demands robust automation and monitoring tools.

In conclusion, cloud hardware and software represent the tangible and intangible elements of cloud computing. Together, they form the foundation and control layer that enables organizations to leverage the power of the cloud. Understanding the interplay between hardware and software is essential for designing, deploying, and managing effective cloud solutions that meet the demands of modern business and technology.

CHAPTER 3

Cloud Service Providers

Cloud service providers are the architects and custodians of the digital transformation that has reshaped industries and empowered businesses worldwide. These titans of technology offer a vast array of services, infrastructure, and platforms that enable organizations to harness the boundless potential of the cloud. In this introduction, we embark on a journey through the realm of cloud service providers, exploring their pivotal role in shaping the modern digital landscape and the diverse solutions they offer to drive innovation, efficiency, and growth. Join us as we unveil the architects of the future and their transformative capabilities in the world of cloud computing.

A. Leading Cloud Providers: AWS, Azure, Google Cloud, and More

In the ever-expanding realm of cloud computing, a few giants have emerged as leaders, offering a vast ecosystem of services and resources to power the digital transformation of businesses worldwide. Amazon Web Services (AWS), Microsoft Azure, and Google Cloud Platform (GCP) are among the top players in this landscape. In this comprehensive analysis, we will delve into the offerings, strengths, and unique features of these leading cloud providers, as well as some notable alternatives.

1. Amazon Web Services (AWS):

Overview: AWS is the pioneer and market leader in cloud computing. Launched in 2006, it has grown to become the most extensive and widely adopted cloud platform globally.

Strengths:

- **Comprehensive Service Portfolio:** AWS offers a vast array of over 200 services, covering computing, storage, databases, machine learning, analytics, and more.

- **Global Reach:** With data centers (Availability Zones) in regions around the world, AWS provides low-latency access and compliance with various data residency requirements.

- **Strong Ecosystem:** AWS has a massive ecosystem of partners, third-party tools, and a robust developer community, making it a top choice for businesses of all sizes.

- **Innovation:** AWS is known for continually innovating and launching new services, including AI/ML (Amazon SageMaker), IoT (AWS IoT Core), and serverless computing (AWS Lambda).

2. Microsoft Azure:

Overview: Microsoft Azure is a cloud computing platform by Microsoft, known for its deep integration with Microsoft products and services.

Strengths:

- **Enterprise Integration:** Azure seamlessly integrates with Microsoft's on-premises products, such as Windows Server and Active Directory, making it a natural choice for enterprises.

- **Hybrid Cloud Solutions:** Azure offers strong hybrid cloud capabilities, allowing organizations to bridge on-premises and cloud environments with tools like Azure Arc.

- **AI and Analytics:** Azure provides a wide range of AI and analytics services, including Azure Machine Learning and Azure Synapse Analytics.

- **Developer Tools:** Azure DevOps and Azure Kubernetes Service (AKS) are popular among developers for building, deploying, and managing applications.

3. Google Cloud Platform (GCP):

Overview: GCP, by Google, is known for its data analytics, machine learning, and container management capabilities.

Strengths:

- **Data and Analytics:** GCP excels in data analytics with BigQuery, Dataflow, and Dataprep. It also offers data storage solutions like Google Cloud Storage.

- **Machine Learning:** Google's expertise in AI and machine learning is evident in GCP's offerings, such as TensorFlow, AI Platform, and AutoML.

- **Container Orchestration:** GCP is the home of Kubernetes, which originated at Google. Google Kubernetes Engine (GKE) is a managed Kubernetes service.

- **Global Network:** GCP leverages Google's extensive global network infrastructure for low-latency, high-performance services.

4. IBM Cloud:

Overview: IBM Cloud offers a broad set of cloud services, including infrastructure, AI, and blockchain, with a focus on hybrid and multicloud deployments.

Strengths:

- **Hybrid Cloud:** IBM's strengths lie in hybrid cloud solutions, such as IBM Cloud Satellite and Red Hat OpenShift, which help bridge on-premises and cloud environments.

- **AI and Quantum Computing:** IBM is a leader in AI research, and its cloud platform features Watson AI services. IBM Quantum provides cloud access to quantum computing resources.

- **Blockchain:** IBM offers blockchain-as-a-service (BaaS) solutions for industries like finance and supply chain.

5. Oracle Cloud:

Overview: Oracle Cloud focuses on cloud infrastructure, databases, and enterprise applications, with a strong presence in the database market.

Strengths:

- **Database Services:** Oracle Cloud offers highly performant and secure database services, including Autonomous Database, which is self-driving, self-securing, and self-repairing.

- **Enterprise Applications:** Oracle Cloud includes a suite of cloud-based enterprise applications, such as Oracle ERP Cloud and Oracle HCM Cloud.

- **Integration:** Oracle Integration Cloud simplifies the integration of on-premises and cloud applications.

6. Alibaba Cloud:

Overview: Alibaba Cloud, also known as Aliyun, is the cloud computing arm of Alibaba Group, the largest e-commerce and tech conglomerate in China.

Strengths:

- **Global Expansion:** Alibaba Cloud has expanded rapidly beyond China, with a global presence that includes data centers in multiple regions.

- **E-commerce Integration:** It offers services tailored for e-commerce, making it a popular choice for businesses in the retail sector.

- **AI and Analytics:** Alibaba Cloud provides AI and analytics solutions, such as MaxCompute and PAI (Platform of Artificial Intelligence).

7. Other Notable Cloud Providers:

- **Salesforce:** Known for its customer relationship management (CRM) platform, Salesforce also offers a range of cloud services and has a strong presence in the software-as-a-service (SaaS) market.

- **Tencent Cloud:** Tencent Cloud is a leading cloud provider in Asia, offering services like cloud computing, AI, and gaming.

- **Rackspace Technology:** Rackspace specializes in managed cloud services, including AWS, Azure, and GCP, providing support and expertise for cloud deployments.

Considerations When Choosing a Cloud Provider:

- **Service Offerings:** Assess your organization's needs and choose a provider that offers the services and features required for your workloads.

- **Pricing and Cost Management:** Compare pricing structures and understand how each provider charges for services to avoid unexpected costs.

- **Compliance and Security:** Ensure the provider complies with industry-specific regulations and provides robust security measures.

- **Integration:** Consider how well the cloud provider integrates with your existing systems and tools.

- **Support and Ecosystem:** Evaluate the level of support, documentation, and community around each cloud provider.

In conclusion, leading cloud providers offer a diverse range of services and solutions, catering to the varying needs of organizations across the globe. The choice of cloud provider depends on factors such as specific use cases, existing technology stack, and strategic goals. Regardless of the provider chosen, cloud computing continues to drive innovation, agility, and digital transformation for businesses of all sizes.

B. Regional and Niche Cloud Providers: Catering to Specialized Needs

While global cloud giants like AWS, Azure, and Google Cloud dominate the cloud computing landscape, a diverse ecosystem of regional and niche cloud providers thrives by offering specialized services, localized support, and unique solutions. In this in-depth analysis, we will explore the world of regional and niche cloud providers, their distinctive strengths, and the markets they serve.

Regional Cloud Providers:

Regional cloud providers focus their services on specific geographic areas or countries, catering to the local needs and regulatory requirements of businesses in those regions. Here are some notable regional cloud providers:

1. **Alibaba Cloud (Aliyun):** While Alibaba Cloud is a major player globally, it has a particularly strong presence in the Asia-Pacific region, serving the specific needs of businesses in China and beyond.

- **Strengths:** Alibaba Cloud offers a range of services tailored to the Asia-Pacific market, including data centers in multiple Asian countries, strong e-commerce integration, and support for Asian languages and currencies.

2. **Tencent Cloud:** Tencent Cloud is a prominent cloud provider in China and Asia, offering cloud computing, AI, gaming, and content delivery services.

- **Strengths:** Tencent Cloud is known for its gaming-related services and partnerships, making it a go-to choice for the gaming industry in Asia.

3. **OVHCloud:** Based in France, OVHCloud is a European cloud provider with data centers across Europe, North America, and Asia.

- **Strengths:** OVHCloud's strengths include its European data sovereignty, strong developer focus, and a comprehensive set of cloud services.

4. **Scaleway:** Scaleway is a European cloud provider with a focus on simplicity and developer-friendly services, including virtual private servers (VPS) and object storage.

- **Strengths:** Scaleway's simple pricing model and European data centers make it a preferred choice for startups and small businesses in Europe.

Niche Cloud Providers:

Niche cloud providers carve out specialized niches by offering services tailored to specific industries, use cases, or technology needs. Here are some examples:

1. **Salesforce:** Salesforce is a leader in the customer relationship management (CRM) industry, providing cloud-based solutions for sales, marketing, service, and more.

- **Strengths:** Salesforce's strength lies in its deep CRM capabilities, making it the go-to choice for businesses seeking to enhance customer engagement.

2. **DigitalOcean:** DigitalOcean specializes in providing cloud infrastructure for developers, offering easy-to-use virtual machines (Droplets) and managed Kubernetes services.

- **Strengths:** DigitalOcean is known for its developer-friendly approach, straightforward pricing, and strong community support.

3. **Rackspace Technology:** Rackspace specializes in managed cloud services, supporting AWS, Azure, Google Cloud, and other cloud providers. It offers expertise in optimizing and managing cloud environments.

- **Strengths:** Rackspace's managed services help organizations navigate the complexities of cloud environments, making it a valuable partner for enterprises.

4. **Heroku:** Heroku is a platform-as-a-service (PaaS) provider that simplifies application deployment and management. It is favored by developers for its ease of use and focus on

application development.

- **Strengths:** Heroku's platform abstracts infrastructure management, allowing developers to focus on coding and application development.

Considerations When Choosing Regional and Niche Providers:

1. **Specialized Services:** Assess whether the provider's services align with your specific industry or use case needs.

2. **Localization:** Consider whether the provider offers localized services, support, and data center presence in regions critical to your business.

3. **Compliance and Regulations:** Verify that the provider complies with local and industry-specific regulations, especially if your business operates in highly regulated sectors.

4. **Scalability:** Ensure that the provider can accommodate your growth and scaling requirements.

5. **Support and Expertise:** Evaluate the level of support, expertise, and community engagement offered by the provider, as these factors can significantly impact your experience.

In conclusion, regional and niche cloud providers fill important niches in the cloud computing landscape. They offer specialized solutions, localized support, and industry-specific expertise, making them valuable alternatives to global cloud giants, especially for businesses with unique needs or operating in specific geographic regions. The choice between global, regional, or niche providers depends on your organization's specific requirements and strategic goals.

C. Comparison of Cloud Services: AWS, Azure, Google Cloud, and More

When selecting a cloud service provider, organizations face a plethora of options, each offering a diverse set of services and features. The decision can be challenging, as it directly impacts an organization's ability to innovate, scale, and manage costs effectively. In this comprehensive comparison, we will dissect the services offered by three major cloud providers—Amazon Web Services (AWS), Microsoft Azure, and Google Cloud Platform (GCP)—and highlight their unique offerings, strengths, and use cases.

Compute Services:

1. **AWS EC2:** Amazon Elastic Compute Cloud (EC2) provides scalable virtual machines (VMs) known as instances. It offers a wide range of instance types, including specialized instances for machine learning and GPU-intensive workloads.

2. **Azure Virtual Machines:** Azure VMs offer various configurations, including Windows and Linux VMs. Azure provides VM scale sets for high availability and Azure Spot VMs for cost savings.

3. **GCP Compute Engine:** Google Compute Engine provides customizable VMs with options for GPUs and custom machine types. It also offers preemptible VMs for cost-effective batch processing.

Container Orchestration:

1. **AWS ECS:** Amazon Elastic Container Service (ECS) is a fully managed container orchestration service for Docker containers.

2. **Azure Kubernetes Service (AKS):** AKS is a managed Kubernetes service for deploying, managing, and scaling containerized applications.

3. **GCP Kubernetes Engine:** Google Kubernetes Engine (GKE) is a managed Kubernetes service known for its strong support for Kubernetes-native features and automated updates.

Serverless Computing:

1. **AWS Lambda:** AWS Lambda allows you to run code in response to events, scaling automatically with no server provisioning required.

2. **Azure Functions:** Azure Functions is a serverless compute service that lets you run event-triggered code without managing infrastructure.

3. **GCP Cloud Functions:** Google Cloud Functions is a serverless execution environment that automatically scales based on incoming traffic.

Database Services:

1. **AWS RDS:** Amazon Relational Database Service (RDS) offers managed relational database services for MySQL, PostgreSQL, SQL Server, and more.

2. **Azure SQL Database:** Azure SQL Database is a fully managed relational database service compatible with SQL Server.

3. **GCP Cloud SQL:** Google Cloud SQL offers managed database services for MySQL, PostgreSQL, and SQL Server.

Big Data and Analytics:

1. **AWS EMR:** Amazon Elastic MapReduce (EMR) is a managed Hadoop and Spark service for big data processing.

2. **Azure HDInsight:** Azure HDInsight offers managed Hadoop, Spark, and other big data analytics services.

3. **GCP BigQuery:** Google BigQuery is a fully managed, serverless data warehouse and analytics platform.

Machine Learning and AI:

1. **AWS SageMaker:** Amazon SageMaker is a fully managed machine learning service that simplifies the development and deployment of machine learning models.

2. **Azure Machine Learning:** Azure Machine Learning is a comprehensive machine learning service with tools for building, training, and deploying models.

3. **GCP AI Platform:** Google Cloud AI Platform provides tools for machine learning model development and deployment, including AutoML for custom machine learning models.

IoT Services:

1. **AWS IoT Core:** AWS IoT Core provides a managed cloud service for connecting IoT devices to the cloud and securely transmitting data.

2. **Azure IoT Hub:** Azure IoT Hub is a fully managed service that enables bi-directional communication between IoT applications and devices.

3. **GCP IoT Core:** Google Cloud IoT Core offers a secure and scalable way to connect and manage IoT devices.

Networking Services:

1. **AWS VPC:** Amazon Virtual Private Cloud (VPC) enables you to create isolated networks within the AWS cloud.

2. **Azure VNet:** Azure Virtual Network (VNet) provides network isolation and connectivity options within Azure.

3. **GCP VPC:** Google Virtual Private Cloud (VPC) offers network isolation and advanced networking features.

Storage Services:

1. **AWS S3:** Amazon Simple Storage Service (S3) is a scalable object storage service with high durability and availability.

2. **Azure Blob Storage:** Azure Blob Storage is an object storage service with tiered storage options.

3. **GCP Cloud Storage:** Google Cloud Storage provides scalable object storage with global availability.

AI and Machine Learning Services:

1. **AWS AI/ML:** AWS offers a wide range of AI/ML services, including Amazon SageMaker for model development and services like Amazon Rekognition for image and video analysis.

2. **Azure AI:** Azure provides AI services, including Azure Machine Learning and Azure Cognitive Services for computer vision, speech recognition, and more.

3. **GCP AI/ML:** Google Cloud offers AI/ML services like AutoML, TensorFlow, and AI Platform for model training and deployment.

Serverless Compute Services:

1. **AWS Lambda:** AWS Lambda allows you to run code in response to events, scaling automatically with no server provisioning required.

2. **Azure Functions:** Azure Functions is a serverless compute service that lets you run event-triggered code without managing infrastructure.

3. **GCP Cloud Functions:** Google Cloud Functions is a serverless execution environment that automatically scales based on incoming traffic.

Comparison Considerations:

- **Service Availability:** Evaluate the availability of services in the regions that are critical to your organization.

- **Pricing Structure:** Understand the pricing models and cost implications of using different services.

- **Integration:** Consider how well services integrate with your existing systems and tools.

- **Scalability and Performance:** Assess the scalability and performance characteristics of services for your workloads.

- **Security and Compliance:** Ensure that the services meet your security and compliance requirements.

In conclusion, the choice of cloud services depends on the specific needs of your organization, your existing technology stack, and your strategic goals. Each cloud provider offers a wide array of services, and understanding the nuances of these offerings is crucial for making informed decisions about which services and providers best suit your business requirements.

D. Vendor Lock-In and Portability in Cloud Computing: Navigating the Complex Landscape

Cloud computing has revolutionized the way organizations manage and deploy their IT resources. However, with the adoption of cloud services, the concerns of vendor lock-in and portability have come to the forefront. In this comprehensive exploration, we will delve into these critical aspects of cloud computing, examining the challenges they pose and strategies for mitigating them.

Vendor Lock-In:

Vendor lock-in occurs when an organization becomes heavily dependent on a specific cloud service provider's proprietary technologies, APIs, and infrastructure. This dependence can make it difficult to migrate to another provider or to bring services back in-house. Here are key considerations regarding vendor lock-in:

Causes of Vendor Lock-In:

1. **Proprietary Services:** Using cloud-specific services and features that are not compatible with other providers can lead to lock-in. For example, AWS Lambda or Azure Functions for serverless computing.

2. **Data Formats and Standards:** Storing data in proprietary formats or relying on non-standard APIs can make data migration challenging.

3. **Orchestration and Automation:** Complex automation scripts or infrastructure as code (IAC) that are tied to a specific provider's environment can create lock-in.

Challenges of Vendor Lock-In:

1. **Migration Complexity:** Transferring workloads, data, and applications to another provider or back on-premises can be time-consuming, costly, and risky.

2. **Cost Implications:** Switching providers may result in additional costs, as organizations may need to rewrite applications and retrain staff.

3. **Loss of Negotiating Power:** The longer an organization remains with a single provider, the less negotiating leverage it may have in contract negotiations.

Strategies to Mitigate Vendor Lock-In:

1. **Multi-Cloud Strategy:** Embrace a multi-cloud approach by using services that are compatible across multiple cloud providers. Kubernetes, for example, is a portable container orchestration platform that runs on AWS, Azure, and Google Cloud.

2. **Use Open Standards:** Adopt open standards and formats for data, such as JSON or CSV, and rely on open-source tools and libraries when possible.

3. **Containerization:** Containerization using technologies like Docker and container orchestration with Kubernetes can abstract the underlying infrastructure, making workloads more portable.

4. **Serverless Abstraction:** Consider serverless frameworks that are not tied to a single provider. Examples include Apache OpenWhisk and AWS SAM (Serverless

Application Model).

Portability:

Portability in cloud computing refers to the ease with which applications, workloads, and data can be moved between different cloud providers or between the cloud and on-premises environments. It ensures that organizations are not locked into a single provider and can maintain flexibility in their cloud strategy.

Key Aspects of Portability:

1. **Data Portability:** The ability to move data in and out of cloud services easily. Use standard data formats and ensure data is not tightly coupled to a specific cloud provider's services.

2. **Application Portability:** Design applications to be platform-agnostic. Utilize containers, serverless, and container orchestration to facilitate application portability.

3. **Infrastructure as Code (IAC):** Implement infrastructure as code practices using tools like Terraform or AWS CloudFormation. This enables the automation and replication of infrastructure across different providers.

4. **Hybrid Cloud:** Consider hybrid cloud architectures that allow workloads to seamlessly move between on-premises and cloud environments.

Common Challenges to Portability:

1. **Diverse Service Offerings:** Different cloud providers offer varying services, making it challenging to find direct equivalents when migrating.

2. **Integration Complexity:** Complex integrations between cloud services may require significant adjustments during migration.

3. **Data Transfer Costs:** The cost of moving large volumes of data between providers can be prohibitive.

4. **Lack of Standardization:** Lack of industry-wide standards for cloud service interoperability can hinder portability efforts.

Strategies to Enhance Portability:

1. **Standardize on Open Technologies:** Adopt open-source tools, standards, and technologies that are compatible with multiple cloud providers.

2. **Design for Portability:** Develop applications with portability in mind, emphasizing the separation of application logic from underlying infrastructure.

3. **Continuous Testing:** Implement continuous testing and validation to ensure applications and workloads remain

portable across different environments.

4. **Multi-Cloud Management Tools:** Utilize multi-cloud management platforms that provide a unified interface for managing workloads across multiple providers.

Conclusion:

Vendor lock-in and portability are two significant challenges organizations face in cloud computing. While achieving complete avoidance of vendor lock-in may be difficult, careful planning and the adoption of best practices can mitigate its impact. Portability, on the other hand, enables organizations to maintain flexibility and choice in their cloud strategies. By embracing a multi-cloud approach, using open standards, and designing for portability, organizations can navigate the complex cloud computing landscape with greater ease and agility.

CHAPTER 4

Cloud Security

As organizations soar to new heights in the cloud, the need for robust cloud security measures becomes paramount. In this introduction, we embark on a journey into the realm of cloud security, where digital assets are protected, data is shielded from threats, and trust is the currency of the cloud. Join us as we explore the critical concepts, best practices, and cutting-edge technologies that form the foundation of cloud security in an era of rapid digital transformation.

A. Cloud Security Models: Protecting the Digital Frontier

Cloud security is a multifaceted discipline that encompasses various models and strategies to safeguard data, applications, and infrastructure in the cloud. These security models serve as the pillars of trust in cloud computing, allowing organizations to harness the benefits of the cloud while mitigating risks. In this comprehensive exploration, we delve into the key cloud security models, their principles, and how they contribute to a secure cloud environment.

1. Shared Responsibility Model:

The shared responsibility model is foundational to cloud security. It delineates the division of security responsibilities between the cloud service provider (CSP) and the customer. Understanding this model is crucial for both parties to ensure that security gaps are addressed effectively.

Responsibilities:

- **CSP Responsibility:** The CSP is responsible for securing the underlying cloud infrastructure, including data centers, physical security, and the hypervisor layer (if using virtualization). They also manage the security of the cloud services themselves, such as databases, storage, and networking.

- **Customer Responsibility:** The customer is responsible for securing their data, applications, and configurations within the cloud. This includes access control, encryption, patch management, and configuring security groups or firewalls.

2. Identity and Access Management (IAM):

IAM is a core component of cloud security that governs user and system access to cloud resources. It ensures that only authorized individuals or systems can interact with cloud services.

Principles:

- **Authentication:** Confirming the identity of users and systems through mechanisms like usernames, passwords, multi-factor authentication (MFA), or identity providers.

- **Authorization:** Defining and enforcing access policies to determine what resources users or systems can access and what actions they can perform.

- **Least Privilege:** Providing the minimum level of access necessary to perform a specific task, reducing the risk of unauthorized access.

3. Data Encryption and Compliance:

Data encryption and compliance are fundamental aspects of cloud security, ensuring that data remains confidential, integrity is maintained, and regulatory requirements are met.

Components:

- **Data Encryption at Rest:** Encrypting data when it's stored in the cloud, making it unreadable without the appropriate decryption keys.

- **Data Encryption in Transit:** Encrypting data while it's being transmitted over networks, safeguarding it from interception.

- **Compliance Frameworks:** Adhering to industry-specific compliance standards, such as GDPR, HIPAA, or PCI DSS, to ensure data protection and privacy.

4. Security Best Practices:

Security best practices encompass a range of guidelines, configurations, and processes aimed at fortifying cloud environments against threats and vulnerabilities.

Examples:

- **Patch Management:** Regularly applying security patches and updates to cloud resources to address known vulnerabilities.

- **Vulnerability Scanning:** Scanning for vulnerabilities within cloud assets and promptly remediating any identified issues.

- **Logging and Monitoring:** Implementing robust logging and monitoring solutions to detect and respond to security incidents in real time.

5. Incident Response and Recovery:

Incident response and recovery plans are essential for mitigating the impact of security incidents and ensuring business continuity in the face of disruptions.

Components:

- **Incident Detection:** Detecting and identifying security incidents, anomalies, or breaches through monitoring and alerting systems.

- **Incident Response:** Defining a structured process for responding to security incidents, including containment, eradication, and recovery steps.

- **Backup and Disaster Recovery:** Implementing data backup and disaster recovery solutions to restore services in the event of data loss or system failures.

6. Security as Code:

Security as code integrates security practices into the DevOps and continuous integration/continuous deployment (CI/CD) pipelines, ensuring that security is built into every stage of the development process.

Principles:

- **Infrastructure as Code (IAC):** Defining cloud resources and configurations using code, enabling automated security checks during resource provisioning.

- **Immutable Infrastructure:** Treating infrastructure as immutable, where changes are replaced rather than modified, reducing the risk of configuration drift and vulnerabilities.

In conclusion, cloud security models serve as the bedrock of a secure cloud environment. They establish the rules, responsibilities, and practices necessary to protect data and systems in the cloud. A well-executed cloud security strategy, built on these models, not only mitigates risks but also fosters trust in the cloud as a secure and reliable platform for innovation and growth.

B. Identity and Access Management (IAM) in Cloud Computing: The Gatekeeper of Digital Trust

Identity and Access Management (IAM) is a critical component of cloud security, serving as the guardian of access privileges, data protection, and overall security in cloud environments. In this comprehensive exploration, we delve into the intricacies of IAM, its fundamental principles, and its pivotal role in ensuring a secure and well-managed cloud ecosystem.

1. Understanding IAM in Cloud Computing:

IAM refers to the practices, technologies, and policies that govern digital identities and their access to cloud resources and data. It revolves around managing the identities of users, systems, and entities involved in cloud operations and controlling their permissions.

Key Components of IAM:

- **Authentication:** The process of verifying the identity of users or systems trying to access cloud resources. Authentication mechanisms include usernames and passwords, multi-factor authentication (MFA), biometrics, and identity providers (e.g., OAuth or SAML).

- **Authorization:** Determining and enforcing what actions and resources users or systems are allowed to access based on their authenticated identity. This process includes defining policies, roles, and permissions.

- **User and Entity Management:** Creating, updating, and deleting user and system accounts, as well as managing their attributes and access privileges.

- **Single Sign-On (SSO):** A centralized authentication process that enables users to log in once and access multiple cloud services without re-entering their credentials.

2. IAM Principles and Best Practices:

Effective IAM in cloud computing relies on several foundational principles and best practices:

- **Least Privilege:** Granting users and systems the

minimum level of access required to perform their roles or tasks. This minimizes the risk of unauthorized actions or data breaches.

- **Role-Based Access Control (RBAC):** Assigning permissions to roles rather than individual users or systems, making it easier to manage and enforce access policies at scale.

- **Segregation of Duties (SoD):** Ensuring that no single user or system has conflicting or excessive access permissions that could lead to security risks.

- **Lifecycle Management:** Automating user and entity provisioning, deprovisioning, and attribute management to ensure timely access adjustments.

- **Audit and Logging:** Implementing robust logging and monitoring to track access activities, detect anomalies, and investigate security incidents.

- **Multi-Factor Authentication (MFA):** Requiring multiple authentication factors, such as something you know (password) and something you have (token or biometric), for heightened security.

- **Identity Federation:** Enabling users to use their existing identities from trusted identity providers to access cloud services, enhancing convenience and security.

3. IAM in Multi-Cloud Environments:

In multi-cloud or hybrid cloud environments, IAM complexity can increase due to the need to manage identities and permissions across multiple cloud providers and on-premises systems. To address this:

- **Single IAM Framework:** Establish a unified IAM framework that spans all cloud platforms and on-premises environments.

- **Federation Standards:** Leverage federation standards like SAML (Security Assertion Markup Language) and OAuth to facilitate seamless identity integration.

- **Cross-Cloud IAM Solutions:** Consider using cross-cloud IAM solutions that provide centralized identity management and policy enforcement.

4. IAM Challenges and Considerations:

While IAM is essential for cloud security, it comes with its own set of challenges and considerations:

- **Complexity:** IAM can become complex as organizations grow and add more cloud services, users, and systems. Robust management tools and automation are crucial.

- **User Experience:** Balancing security with a positive

user experience is critical to prevent security measures from hindering productivity.

- **Scalability:** IAM solutions must scale to accommodate a growing number of users and devices.

- **Integration:** Ensuring seamless integration with various cloud services, APIs, and legacy systems can be challenging.

- **Compliance:** Meeting industry-specific compliance requirements (e.g., GDPR, HIPAA) is essential when handling sensitive data.

In conclusion, IAM is the linchpin of cloud security, ensuring that the right people and systems have access to the right resources while protecting sensitive data and mitigating risks. A well-designed and diligently managed IAM strategy is essential for building trust in cloud computing and safeguarding the digital assets of organizations in an increasingly connected and dynamic digital landscape.

C. Data Encryption and Compliance in Cloud Computing: Fortifying Digital Trust

In the ever-evolving landscape of cloud computing, data encryption and compliance stand as twin pillars of security, safeguarding sensitive information and ensuring regulatory adherence. This in-depth exploration delves into the intricate world of data encryption and compliance in the cloud, examining their critical roles, best practices, and the symbiotic relationship they share.

Data Encryption in the Cloud:

Data encryption is the practice of converting data into a ciphertext format that can only be deciphered by individuals or systems possessing the appropriate decryption keys. In the cloud, encryption serves as a crucial safeguard against unauthorized access, data breaches, and data theft. Here are key facets of data encryption in cloud computing:

1. Types of Data Encryption:

- **Data at Rest Encryption:** Encrypting data when it is stored in cloud repositories, such as databases or object storage. Encrypted data remains protected even if physical storage devices are compromised.

- **Data in Transit Encryption:** Encrypting data as it traverses networks between the cloud and end-users, ensuring that data remains confidential during transmission. Transport Layer Security (TLS) and Secure Sockets Layer (SSL) are common protocols for securing data in transit.

2. Encryption Key Management:

Effective encryption requires robust key management practices to securely generate, store, rotate, and distribute encryption keys. Key management systems (KMS) or hardware security modules (HSMs) are often used to manage encryption keys in the cloud.

3. Client-Side Encryption:

In client-side encryption, data is encrypted on the client's side before being uploaded to the cloud. This approach ensures that data is encrypted even before it reaches cloud servers, providing an additional layer of security.

4. Zero-Knowledge Encryption:

Zero-knowledge encryption is a concept where service providers have no knowledge of the encryption keys or the plaintext data. Only the data owner possesses the keys. This ensures that even service providers cannot access the data.

5. Compliance and Encryption:

Many compliance standards, such as the Health Insurance Portability and Accountability Act (HIPAA) and the General Data Protection Regulation (GDPR), mandate the use of encryption to protect sensitive data. Encryption helps organizations meet regulatory requirements and avoid hefty fines.

Compliance in the Cloud:

Compliance in cloud computing refers to adhering to industry-specific or regional regulations, standards, and best practices that govern the handling and protection of sensitive data. Compliance is crucial for maintaining trust and legal standing, especially when dealing with sensitive data or customer information. Here are key aspects of compliance in the cloud:

1. Regulatory Compliance:

Different industries and regions have their own compliance requirements. Examples include:

- **HIPAA:** Ensuring that healthcare data remains confidential and secure.
- **GDPR:** Protecting the privacy and data rights of European Union citizens.
- **PCI DSS:** Safeguarding credit card data to prevent fraud.
- **SOC 2:** Assessing the security, availability, processing integrity, confidentiality, and privacy of customer data.

2. Compliance Auditing:

Organizations must regularly undergo compliance audits to assess their adherence to regulatory requirements. These audits may be performed by internal teams or external auditors.

3. Data Classification:

Classifying data based on its sensitivity and importance is a foundational step in compliance. It helps organizations apply appropriate security measures, such as encryption, to protect sensitive data.

4. Compliance as Code:

In cloud-native environments, organizations can implement compliance as code (CaC) to automate and enforce compliance policies throughout the development and deployment lifecycle.

5. Cloud Service Provider (CSP) Compliance:

CSPs often provide compliance documentation, known as attestation reports, to demonstrate their adherence to various standards and regulations. Customers can use these reports to assess the security posture of their cloud providers.

The Symbiotic Relationship: Data Encryption and Compliance:

Data encryption and compliance share a symbiotic relationship in cloud computing:

- **Encryption Supports Compliance:** Strong encryption is often a fundamental requirement of compliance standards. It helps protect data from unauthorized access and breaches.

- **Compliance Drives Encryption Adoption:** Compliance regulations mandate encryption to protect sensitive data. Organizations must implement encryption solutions to meet these requirements.

- **Encryption Eases Compliance Audits:** Properly implemented encryption can simplify compliance audits by demonstrating that sensitive data is adequately protected.

- **Data Classification Enhances Both:** Accurate data classification supports encryption efforts and ensures that compliance requirements are met for sensitive data.

In conclusion, data encryption and compliance are intertwined elements of cloud security, working together to protect sensitive information, maintain regulatory compliance, and build trust in cloud environments. Organizations must carefully plan and implement encryption strategies while adhering to relevant compliance standards to navigate the complex landscape of cloud computing securely and responsibly.

D. Security Best Practices in Cloud Computing: Safeguarding the Digital Frontier

In the rapidly evolving world of cloud computing, security best practices serve as the guiding principles that enable organizations to navigate the digital landscape while protecting their assets and data. This comprehensive exploration delves into the core principles, strategies, and tactics that form the foundation of security best practices in cloud computing.

1. Embrace the Principle of Least Privilege (PoLP):

Principle: Least Privilege dictates that users, systems, and processes should have only the minimum level of access and permissions necessary to perform their roles or tasks.

Application: Apply the principle of least privilege to cloud resources, user accounts, and systems to minimize the risk of unauthorized access or accidental data exposure. Implement role-based access control (RBAC) to assign permissions at a granular level.

2. Implement Robust Authentication and Authorization:

Authentication: Verify the identities of users, systems, and entities trying to access cloud resources through mechanisms such as passwords, multi-factor authentication (MFA), biometrics, and single sign-on (SSO).

Authorization: Define and enforce access policies that determine what actions and resources users or systems can access based on their authenticated identity. Ensure that access controls are properly configured to prevent unauthorized actions.

3. Regularly Update and Patch Systems:

Principle: Regularly applying security patches and updates to cloud resources and underlying systems is essential to address known vulnerabilities.

Application: Implement a robust patch management process to keep cloud resources up to date. Use automation tools to streamline the patching process and reduce exposure to vulnerabilities.

4. Employ Vulnerability Scanning and Assessment:

Principle: Regularly scan cloud assets and infrastructure for vulnerabilities to identify and remediate security weaknesses.

Application: Use vulnerability scanning tools to assess cloud environments for potential security risks. Prioritize and remediate vulnerabilities based on their severity and impact.

5. Enable Robust Logging and Monitoring:

Principle: Implement comprehensive logging and monitoring to detect and respond to security incidents in real time.

Application: Set up centralized logging solutions to collect and analyze logs from cloud resources. Implement alerting mechanisms to notify security teams of suspicious activities or anomalies.

6. Encrypt Data at Rest and in Transit:

Principle: Encrypt data both when it's stored (data at rest) and when it's transmitted over networks (data in transit) to protect it from unauthorized access.

Application: Utilize encryption mechanisms provided by cloud service providers for data at rest and deploy secure communication protocols such as TLS/SSL for data in transit. Manage encryption keys securely.

7. Educate and Train Personnel:

Principle: Security awareness and training are crucial for ensuring that employees and teams understand security risks and best practices.

Application: Provide regular security training to employees and contractors. Foster a culture of security awareness to mitigate the human factor in security breaches.

8. Implement Multi-Factor Authentication (MFA):

Principle: Multi-factor authentication adds an extra layer of security by requiring users to provide multiple forms of verification before granting access.

Application: Enforce MFA for user accounts accessing cloud resources, especially for privileged or sensitive accounts. This greatly reduces the risk of unauthorized access due to stolen or compromised credentials.

9. Employ Security as Code (SaC):

Principle: Integrate security practices into the development and deployment pipelines using automation and code-based security policies.

Application: Implement security as code (SaC) practices such as infrastructure as code (IaC) and continuous security testing to automate security checks throughout the software development lifecycle.

10. Conduct Regular Security Audits and Assessments:

Principle: Periodically assess the security posture of cloud resources and environments through security audits and assessments.

Application: Engage in security audits and assessments to identify weaknesses, assess compliance with security standards, and improve overall security.

11. Prepare and Test Incident Response Plans:

Principle: Develop incident response plans to address security incidents effectively and minimize their impact.

Application: Create incident response plans that outline procedures for detecting, reporting, and responding to security incidents. Conduct tabletop exercises and simulations to test the effectiveness of these plans.

12. Automate Security Compliance Checks:

Principle: Automate compliance checks and validations to ensure that cloud resources adhere to security policies and standards.

Application: Use automated compliance monitoring tools to continuously assess and enforce security policies. Automatically remediate non-compliant resources.

In conclusion, security best practices are the bedrock of a secure cloud computing environment. They provide organizations with the guidance and strategies needed to protect their digital assets, maintain regulatory compliance, and build trust in an increasingly interconnected and dynamic digital landscape. Implementing these best practices is essential for safeguarding data, systems, and applications in the cloud.

E. Incident Response and Recovery in Cloud Computing: Safeguarding Business Continuity

Incident response and recovery (IR&R) is a critical aspect of cloud security, ensuring that organizations can effectively detect, respond to, and recover from security incidents in cloud environments. In this comprehensive exploration, we delve into the intricacies of incident response and recovery, covering key principles, best practices, and strategies for maintaining business continuity in the cloud.

Incident Response in Cloud Computing:

1. Detection and Identification:

- **Event Monitoring:** Establish comprehensive event monitoring and alerting systems to detect anomalous activities or potential security incidents. This includes monitoring logs, network traffic, and user behavior.

- **Incident Classification:** Classify detected events and incidents based on severity and impact to prioritize response efforts. Incident classification helps in allocating resources appropriately.

2. Incident Containment and Eradication:

- **Isolation:** Contain the incident by isolating affected systems or resources to prevent further damage or data breaches. This may involve isolating compromised virtual machines or services.

- **Eradication:** Identify and remove the root cause of the incident. This step involves eliminating the source of the compromise and securing affected systems.

3. Communication and Reporting:

- **Internal Communication:** Establish clear communication channels within the organization to ensure that incident response teams, management, and relevant stakeholders are informed about the incident.

- **External Reporting:** In some cases, incidents may require external reporting to regulatory bodies, law enforcement, or customers, depending on legal and contractual obligations.

4. Recovery and Remediation:

- **Resource Restoration:** Once the incident is contained and eradicated, begin the process of resource restoration. Restore affected systems and services to their normal operation.

- **Patch and Remediate:** Implement security patches, updates, and configuration changes to prevent similar incidents in the future. Perform post-incident reviews and lessons learned sessions to identify areas for improvement.

Incident Recovery in Cloud Computing:

1. Backup and Disaster Recovery:

- **Data Backup:** Regularly back up critical data and

configurations in the cloud. Cloud providers often offer backup services or snapshots that can be used for data recovery.

- **Disaster Recovery Plans:** Develop disaster recovery plans that outline procedures for recovering cloud resources and services in the event of data loss, system failures, or catastrophic incidents.

2. Redundancy and High Availability:

- **Redundant Architectures:** Design cloud architectures with redundancy and failover capabilities to ensure high availability. This helps minimize downtime during incidents.

- **Load Balancing:** Implement load balancing to distribute traffic across multiple instances or regions, ensuring continued service availability even if one component fails.

3. Data Encryption and Isolation:

- **Data Encryption:** Utilize encryption for data at rest and in transit to protect sensitive information. Encryption helps prevent data exposure in the event of a security incident.

- **Network Isolation:** Implement network segmentation and isolation to contain incidents and prevent lateral movement by attackers.

4. Incident Simulation and Testing:

- **Tabletop Exercises:** Conduct tabletop exercises and simulations to test incident response and recovery plans. These exercises help identify weaknesses and improve response processes.

- **Red Team Testing:** Employ ethical hacking and penetration testing to assess the readiness of cloud environments to withstand cyberattacks and security incidents.

5. Cloud Service Provider (CSP) Support:

- **CSP Incident Response:** Familiarize yourself with the incident response capabilities and support provided by your cloud service provider. Understand their roles and responsibilities in the event of a security incident.

- **SLAs and Agreements:** Ensure that service level agreements (SLAs) with your CSP include provisions for incident response and recovery, including response times and responsibilities.

6. Continuous Monitoring and Logging:

- **Continuous Monitoring:** Implement continuous monitoring of cloud resources and services to detect security incidents in real time.

- **Logging and Auditing:** Maintain detailed logs and audit trails of activities in the cloud environment. These logs are invaluable for incident investigation and forensic analysis.

In conclusion, incident response and recovery are integral components of cloud security and business continuity. A well-defined incident response plan, coupled with effective recovery strategies, ensures that organizations can detect, respond to, and recover from security incidents, minimizing downtime and data loss. By following best practices and continuously improving incident response and recovery capabilities, organizations can safeguard their cloud environments and maintain operational resilience in the face of evolving cyber threats.

CHAPTER 5

Cloud Networking

Cloud networking is the central nervous system of modern IT infrastructure, enabling organizations to connect, communicate, and collaborate across the digital landscape. In this introduction, we embark on a journey through the intricacies of cloud networking, where virtual networks, high-speed data highways, and innovative protocols form the backbone of the digital age. Join us as we explore the vital role cloud networking plays in shaping the interconnected world of cloud computing.

A. Virtual Private Cloud (VPC) in Cloud Computing: Crafting Secure and Isolated Network Environments

Virtual Private Cloud (VPC) is a fundamental component of cloud networking that allows organizations to create isolated and customizable network environments within a cloud service provider's infrastructure. VPCs serve as the foundation for building secure, segmented, and highly available cloud architectures. In this in-depth exploration, we dive into the concept, architecture, benefits, and best practices of Virtual Private Clouds.

1. Understanding Virtual Private Cloud (VPC):

Definition: A Virtual Private Cloud (VPC) is a logically isolated network space within a cloud service provider's data center, where organizations can provision and manage their virtualized network resources, such as virtual machines (VMs), subnets, and network gateways.

Key Components of VPC:

- **Subnets:** Subnets are address ranges within a VPC that allow organizations to segment their network into smaller, manageable parts. Subnets can be public or private, depending on their accessibility from the internet.

- **Route Tables:** Route tables define the routing paths for network traffic within the VPC. They determine how traffic is forwarded between subnets and out to the internet.

- **Network Access Control Lists (NACLs):** NACLs act as stateless firewalls, controlling inbound and outbound traffic at the subnet level based on rules defined by administrators.

- **Security Groups:** Security groups are stateful firewalls that control traffic at the instance level. They define rules to allow or deny specific types of traffic to and from instances within a subnet.

- **Internet Gateways (IGWs):** IGWs enable

communication between resources within a VPC and the public internet. They serve as a bridge between private and public subnets.

2. VPC Architecture:

A typical VPC architecture consists of the following components:

- **VPC:** The root network environment that spans one or more availability zones (AZs) within a cloud region.
- **Subnets:** Organized within the VPC, subnets can be public (accessible from the internet) or private (isolated from the internet).
- **Route Tables:** Each subnet is associated with a route table that directs traffic within the VPC.
- **Internet Gateway (IGW):** Allows resources in public subnets to communicate with the public internet.
- **NAT Gateway:** Permits instances in private subnets to initiate outbound traffic to the internet while preventing unsolicited inbound traffic.
- **Virtual Private Network (VPN) or Direct Connect:** Securely connects on-premises data centers to the VPC for hybrid cloud deployments.

3. Benefits of Virtual Private Cloud (VPC):

a. Isolation and Segmentation:

- **Security:** VPCs enable network isolation, allowing organizations to create distinct security boundaries for different applications and services.

- **Compliance:** Segmentation supports regulatory compliance by ensuring that sensitive data remains isolated from less secure environments.

b. Scalability:

- **Resource Scaling:** VPCs can scale resources horizontally and vertically, accommodating growing workloads and traffic demands.

- **Availability Zones:** VPCs can span multiple availability zones, enhancing fault tolerance and high availability.

c. Cost Efficiency:

- **Resource Allocation:** VPCs allow organizations to allocate resources efficiently, reducing infrastructure costs.

- **Pay-as-You-Go:** Cloud providers typically charge for VPC resources on a pay-as-you-go basis, reducing upfront capital expenditures.

d. Connectivity:

- **Internet Access:** VPCs can provide internet connectivity for public-facing resources while maintaining private networks for internal services.

- **Hybrid Cloud:** VPCs facilitate secure connections between on-premises data centers and cloud resources.

4. Best Practices for Virtual Private Cloud (VPC) Management:

- **Planning:** Careful planning of VPC architecture, including subnet design, IP address management, and routing, is crucial for scalability and security.

- **Security:** Implement security groups, NACLs, and other security measures to control traffic and protect resources.

- **Monitoring and Logging:** Use cloud-native monitoring and logging tools to gain visibility into VPC traffic and resource performance.

- **Backup and Disaster Recovery:** Establish backup and disaster recovery strategies for critical VPC resources.

- **Documentation:** Maintain detailed documentation of VPC configurations, including routing tables, security groups, and subnet definitions.

Conclusion:

Virtual Private Cloud (VPC) is an essential building block in cloud computing, providing organizations with the flexibility, security, and scalability needed to create complex network architectures. When properly designed and managed, VPCs empower businesses to harness the full potential of cloud resources while maintaining the integrity and security of their network environments.

B. Content Delivery Networks (CDNs) in Cloud Computing: Accelerating Digital Content Delivery

Content Delivery Networks (CDNs) play a pivotal role in modern cloud computing by optimizing the distribution and delivery of digital content to users around the world. They enhance website performance, reduce latency, and ensure the availability of web applications and media content. In this comprehensive exploration, we delve into the concept, architecture, benefits, and best practices of CDNs.

1. Understanding Content Delivery Networks (CDNs):

Definition: A Content Delivery Network (CDN) is a distributed network of geographically dispersed servers strategically positioned to accelerate the delivery of web content, applications, and media to end-users. CDNs work by caching and serving content from locations closer to users, reducing the latency and load on origin servers.

Key Components of CDNs:

- **Edge Servers:** These are the distributed servers located in various geographic locations, also known as points of presence (PoPs). Edge servers store cached copies of content and serve them to users.

- **Content Caching:** CDNs cache static and dynamic content, including images, videos, scripts, and HTML pages, to reduce the need for repeated requests to origin servers.

- **Anycast Routing:** CDNs use anycast routing to direct user requests to the nearest edge server based on network proximity, reducing latency.

- **Load Balancing:** CDNs employ load balancing algorithms to distribute user requests evenly across multiple edge servers, ensuring optimal resource utilization.

2. CDN Architecture:

A typical CDN architecture consists of the following components:

- **Origin Server:** The origin server is the original source of content, where web assets are hosted. CDNs pull content from the origin server and cache it in edge servers.

- **Edge Servers:** These servers are strategically located in data centers worldwide. They store cached content and serve it to users based on their geographic proximity.

- **Content Distribution:** CDNs use various algorithms to distribute content efficiently, considering factors like server health, location, and load.

- **Request Routing:** When a user requests content, the CDN's request routing mechanism directs the request to the nearest edge server.

3. Benefits of Content Delivery Networks (CDNs):

a. Improved Performance:

- **Reduced Latency:** CDNs deliver content from servers closer to users, significantly reducing latency and improving load times.

- **High Availability:** CDNs ensure content availability even during traffic spikes or server outages by distributing the load across multiple servers.

b. Enhanced Scalability:

- **Global Reach:** CDNs can scale content delivery to a

global audience, providing a consistent user experience regardless of location.

- **Traffic Offloading:** By caching content at edge locations, CDNs offload traffic from origin servers, reducing their workload and preventing overloads.

c. Cost Efficiency:

- **Reduced Bandwidth Costs:** CDNs optimize data transfer, leading to reduced bandwidth costs for both organizations and users.

d. Security:

- **DDoS Mitigation:** CDNs often include distributed denial of service (DDoS) protection, mitigating attacks before they reach origin servers.

- **Web Application Firewall (WAF):** Some CDNs offer WAF services to protect web applications from common security threats.

4. Best Practices for CDN Deployment:

- **Content Caching Strategy:** Tailor your caching strategy to balance cache expiration times for dynamic content and long-term caching for static assets.

- **Geographic Coverage:** Choose a CDN provider with

a broad geographic presence to ensure efficient content delivery worldwide.

- **Performance Monitoring:** Continuously monitor CDN performance to identify bottlenecks or latency issues.

- **HTTPS Support:** Ensure that your CDN supports HTTPS for secure content delivery.

- **Security:** Leverage the security features provided by your CDN to protect against DDoS attacks and other threats.

Conclusion:

Content Delivery Networks (CDNs) are indispensable tools in the cloud computing landscape, enhancing the performance, availability, and security of web applications and digital content. By strategically deploying CDNs and optimizing their configurations, organizations can provide users with fast, reliable, and secure access to their online assets, ultimately delivering an exceptional digital experience.

C. Cloud Networking Protocols: The Communication Backbone of Cloud Computing

Cloud networking protocols are the digital highways that enable data transmission and communication between various cloud components, services, and users. These protocols play a fundamental role in ensuring the reliability, security, and efficiency of cloud networks. In this comprehensive exploration, we delve into the world of cloud networking protocols, covering key concepts, popular protocols, and their critical importance in modern cloud computing.

1. The Role of Cloud Networking Protocols:

Definition: Cloud networking protocols are a set of rules and conventions that govern how data is transmitted, received, and processed within cloud environments. They facilitate communication between cloud resources, data centers, and users, ensuring the seamless flow of information.

Key Functions:

- **Data Transport:** Cloud networking protocols facilitate the transmission of data between cloud servers, client devices, and other network elements.

- **Resource Discovery:** Some protocols assist in the discovery of cloud resources, enabling applications and services to locate and interact with them.

- **Security:** Protocols often include encryption and authentication mechanisms to secure data in transit and protect against unauthorized access.

2. Popular Cloud Networking Protocols:

a. Transmission Control Protocol (TCP):

TCP is a connection-oriented protocol that provides reliable, ordered, and error-checked data transmission. It ensures that data sent from one point to another arrives intact and in the correct order. TCP is commonly used for web browsing, email, and file transfers.

b. Internet Protocol (IP):

IP is responsible for addressing and routing packets of data so that they can travel across networks and arrive at their destination. IPv4 and IPv6 are the two main versions of the Internet Protocol. IP forms the basis for most internet communication.

c. Hypertext Transfer Protocol (HTTP) and HTTP Secure (HTTPS):

HTTP is used for transferring web content, such as web pages and multimedia, between a client (e.g., a web browser) and a web server. HTTPS, a secure version of HTTP, encrypts data to protect it from eavesdropping and tampering.

d. Border Gateway Protocol (BGP):

BGP is a routing protocol that plays a crucial role in internet and cloud networking by determining the best path for data to traverse the internet. It enables routers to make dynamic decisions on how to route traffic based on various factors.

e. Simple Network Management Protocol (SNMP):

SNMP is used for managing and monitoring network devices, including routers, switches, and servers. It allows administrators to collect information and configure network components remotely.

f. Virtual Extensible LAN (VXLAN) and Generic Routing Encapsulation (GRE):

These are tunneling protocols used in virtualized and cloud environments to encapsulate and transmit packets across networks. They are essential for creating virtual networks and isolating traffic within cloud environments.

3. Importance of Cloud Networking Protocols:

a. Scalability: Protocols support the dynamic scaling of cloud resources and services, accommodating growing workloads and user demands.

b. Reliability: Cloud networking protocols ensure data is transmitted reliably, minimizing packet loss and data corruption.

c. Security: Many protocols include encryption and authentication mechanisms to safeguard data and protect against cyber threats.

d. Interoperability: Cloud networking protocols enable diverse cloud services and components to work together seamlessly, regardless of their underlying infrastructure or technology stack.

e. Performance: Efficient protocols optimize data transmission, reducing latency and improving overall network performance.

4. Challenges and Considerations:

a. Security: The secure transmission of data is paramount, especially in cloud environments where sensitive information is often processed and stored.

b. Protocol Compatibility: Ensuring that different cloud components and services can communicate effectively may require careful protocol selection and configuration.

c. Quality of Service (QoS): Meeting performance requirements, such as low latency and high throughput, often depends on QoS mechanisms implemented through protocols.

d. Network Monitoring: Proper monitoring tools and practices are essential to detect and troubleshoot issues related to cloud networking protocols.

Conclusion:

Cloud networking protocols serve as the underlying infrastructure that enables the seamless operation of cloud services, applications, and data transmission. These protocols play a vital role in the reliability, security, and performance of cloud networks, making them a cornerstone of modern cloud computing. Understanding and optimizing the use of these protocols is essential for organizations to harness the full potential of cloud technology while ensuring a safe and efficient digital experience.

D. Hybrid and Multi-Cloud Networking: Bridging the Digital Divide

Hybrid and multi-cloud networking are strategic approaches that empower organizations to harness the advantages of multiple cloud environments, whether public, private, or a combination of both. These networking paradigms enable seamless communication and data transfer across diverse cloud resources. In this comprehensive exploration, we delve into the concepts, architectures, benefits, and best practices of hybrid and multi-cloud networking.

1. Understanding Hybrid and Multi-Cloud Networking:

a. Hybrid Cloud:

Definition: Hybrid cloud refers to an integrated cloud

environment that combines on-premises infrastructure (private cloud) with one or more public cloud services. It allows data and applications to move between private and public clouds as needed.

b. Multi-Cloud:

Definition: Multi-cloud involves using two or more cloud providers to host different workloads or services. These cloud providers can be public, private, or a combination, and they may serve various purposes within an organization's cloud strategy.

Key Concepts:

- **Interoperability:** Hybrid and multi-cloud environments aim to enable seamless communication, data exchange, and resource orchestration across disparate cloud platforms.

- **Resource Mobility:** These approaches facilitate the movement of workloads and data between on-premises and cloud environments, between different public clouds, and even between public and private clouds.

2. Architecture of Hybrid and Multi-Cloud Networking:

a. Hybrid Cloud Architecture:

- **Private Cloud:** This is typically an organization's on-premises infrastructure or a dedicated cloud environment. It can host sensitive data and applications requiring strict control.

- **Public Cloud:** Public cloud providers offer scalable and cost-effective resources that can be used for specific workloads or applications. These resources are accessible via the internet.

- **Connectivity:** To establish hybrid cloud connectivity, organizations use dedicated network connections, virtual private networks (VPNs), or direct connections provided by cloud providers.

b. Multi-Cloud Architecture:

- **Multiple Cloud Providers:** An organization may choose different cloud providers (e.g., AWS, Azure, Google Cloud) to host specific services or applications based on their strengths and features.

- **Orchestration Layer:** An orchestration layer or management platform is used to coordinate resources, workloads, and data across different cloud providers. Kubernetes and Terraform are examples of such tools.

3. Benefits of Hybrid and Multi-Cloud Networking:

a. Flexibility and Agility:

- **Workload Optimization:** Organizations can deploy

workloads in the cloud that best suits their specific requirements, whether public or private.

- **Resource Scaling:** Hybrid and multi-cloud setups allow organizations to scale resources up or down as needed to meet changing demands.

b. Risk Mitigation:

- **Disaster Recovery:** Hybrid and multi-cloud setups enhance data redundancy and disaster recovery capabilities by distributing data across multiple locations.

- **Vendor Lock-In Mitigation:** Organizations can reduce dependency on a single cloud provider, mitigating the risk of vendor lock-in.

c. Cost Efficiency:

- **Cost Optimization:** By leveraging different cloud providers, organizations can optimize costs by selecting the most cost-effective options for their workloads.

- **Pricing Negotiation:** The ability to negotiate pricing with multiple providers can lead to favorable terms and cost savings.

d. Geographic Reach:

- **Global Presence:** Multi-cloud networking enables

organizations to host services and data in various regions to provide low-latency access to users worldwide.

4. Best Practices for Hybrid and Multi-Cloud Networking:

- **Security and Compliance:** Ensure that security policies and compliance measures are consistent across all cloud environments.

- **Standardized Networking Protocols:** Use standardized networking protocols and technologies to enable seamless communication between cloud environments.

- **Automation and Orchestration:** Implement automation and orchestration tools to simplify workload deployment and management.

- **Monitoring and Visibility:** Utilize cloud management and monitoring tools to gain visibility into the performance and security of your hybrid and multi-cloud setup.

Conclusion:

Hybrid and multi-cloud networking represent powerful strategies for organizations looking to optimize their cloud infrastructure, increase agility, and enhance resilience. These approaches enable seamless communication and resource mobility across diverse cloud environments, offering flexibility, cost efficiency, and risk mitigation. By following best practices and effectively managing the complexity of hybrid and multi-cloud networking, organizations can maximize the benefits of their cloud investments and thrive in the digital era.

E. Performance Optimization in Cloud Computing: Accelerating the Digital Experience

Performance optimization in cloud computing is a critical aspect of ensuring that cloud resources and applications deliver fast, reliable, and efficient services to users. It involves a comprehensive approach that includes fine-tuning various components of the cloud environment, from infrastructure and network configurations to application code and data management. In this in-depth exploration, we delve into the key concepts, strategies, and best practices for optimizing performance in the cloud.

1. Understanding Performance Optimization:

Definition: Performance optimization in cloud computing refers to the systematic process of enhancing the speed, responsiveness, and efficiency of cloud-based services and applications. It encompasses a wide range of techniques and strategies aimed at eliminating bottlenecks, reducing latency, and maximizing resource utilization.

Key Components of Performance Optimization:

- **Infrastructure Optimization:** Tuning the underlying cloud infrastructure, including virtual machines, storage, and network configurations, to achieve optimal resource allocation and utilization.

- **Application Optimization:** Enhancing the performance of cloud-native or third-party applications by optimizing code, database queries, and resource usage.

- **Network Optimization:** Optimizing network configurations and protocols to reduce latency and improve data transfer speeds within and between cloud regions.

2. Performance Optimization Strategies:

a. Infrastructure Optimization:

- **Resource Scaling:** Implement auto-scaling to dynamically adjust resource allocation based on workload demands. This ensures that resources are available when needed and scaled down during periods of lower demand, optimizing cost and performance.

- **Load Balancing:** Distribute incoming traffic evenly across multiple instances or resources to prevent overloading and improve response times.

- **Caching:** Utilize caching mechanisms to store frequently accessed data, reducing the need to fetch data from the source every time, and subsequently reducing latency.

b. Application Optimization:

- **Code Profiling:** Use profiling tools to identify performance bottlenecks in application code. Optimize code by eliminating inefficiencies, reducing CPU usage, and minimizing memory consumption.

- **Database Optimization:** Optimize database queries, indexing, and data retrieval techniques to reduce database latency and improve response times.

- **Content Delivery:** Leverage Content Delivery Networks (CDNs) to cache and deliver static content, reducing the load on application servers and improving content delivery speed.

c. Network Optimization:

- **Content Compression:** Implement data compression techniques to reduce the size of data transmitted over the network, resulting in faster data transfers.

- **Quality of Service (QoS):** Implement QoS policies to prioritize critical network traffic, ensuring that essential applications receive the necessary bandwidth and minimizing delays.

- **Minimize Round Trips:** Reduce the number of round trips between client and server by consolidating requests and responses, thereby minimizing network latency.

3. Best Practices for Performance Optimization:

- **Regular Monitoring:** Continuously monitor cloud resources and application performance using cloud-native monitoring tools and third-party solutions. Set up alerts for abnormal behavior.

- **Benchmarking:** Conduct performance benchmarking to establish baseline metrics and track improvements over time.

- **Scalability Testing:** Perform load testing and scalability testing to ensure that the cloud infrastructure can handle peak workloads without degradation in performance.

- **Security Considerations:** Optimize security measures, but be mindful of their impact on performance. Find a balance between security and performance requirements.

- **Regular Updates:** Keep all components of the cloud environment, including operating systems, applications, and libraries, up to date to take advantage of performance improvements and security patches.

4. The Role of Cloud Service Providers (CSPs):

Cloud service providers like AWS, Azure, and Google Cloud offer a range of tools and services for performance optimization. These may include load balancing services, auto-scaling capabilities, and managed database services designed to optimize performance automatically.

Conclusion:

Performance optimization is a continuous and iterative process in cloud computing. By implementing the right strategies, best practices, and tools, organizations can deliver fast, reliable, and efficient cloud-based services to their users, ultimately enhancing the digital experience and achieving business success in the cloud era.

CHAPTER 6

Cloud Computing Architectures

Cloud computing architectures lay the foundation for the digital transformation of organizations, offering a structured and flexible framework to design, deploy, and manage cloud-based services and applications. These architectures encompass a diverse spectrum of models and technologies, from microservices and serverless computing to container orchestration and cloud-native solutions. In this introductory exploration, we embark on a journey into the realm of cloud computing architectures, where innovation and scalability converge to reshape the digital landscape.

A. Microservices and Serverless Computing: Revolutionizing Cloud Architectures

Microservices and serverless computing are two groundbreaking paradigms within cloud computing architectures that have redefined how applications are built, deployed, and managed. These architectural approaches break down monolithic applications into smaller, more manageable components and enable organizations to build scalable, resilient, and cost-efficient solutions. In this in-depth exploration, we delve into the concepts, principles, benefits, and challenges of microservices and serverless computing.

1. Microservices Architecture:

a. Definition: Microservices is an architectural style that structures an application as a collection of loosely coupled, independently deployable services. Each service focuses on a specific business capability and communicates with others via APIs or lightweight protocols.

b. Key Concepts:

- **Service Independence:** Microservices are independently developed, deployed, and scaled. A change or failure in one service does not necessarily impact others.

- **Decentralized Data Management:** Each microservice can have its own data store, tailored to its specific requirements, such as relational or NoSQL databases.

- **Polyglot Architecture:** Microservices allow the use of different programming languages, frameworks, and technologies for each service, optimizing for the specific task.

c. Benefits:

- **Scalability:** Individual services can be scaled independently, ensuring optimal resource utilization.

- **Faster Development:** Smaller, focused teams can develop and release services more rapidly, leading to faster time-to-market.

- **Resilience:** Isolation between services means that a failure in one service doesn't necessarily cause system-wide outages.

- **Flexibility:** Microservices architecture enables technology stack flexibility, allowing organizations to choose the best tools for each service.

d. Challenges:

- **Complexity:** Managing a distributed system of microservices can be complex, requiring robust service discovery, orchestration, and monitoring.

- **Data Consistency:** Ensuring data consistency across services can be challenging when each service has its own data store.

- **Testing and Debugging:** Testing and debugging in a distributed environment can be more complex than in a monolithic application.

2. Serverless Computing:

a. Definition: Serverless computing, often referred to as

Function-as-a-Service (FaaS), is an execution model where cloud providers automatically manage the infrastructure needed to run code. Developers focus solely on writing functions or small pieces of code that execute in response to events.

b. Key Concepts:

- **Event-Driven:** Serverless functions are triggered by events, such as HTTP requests, database changes, or file uploads.

- **Stateless:** Functions are stateless and ephemeral, meaning they do not maintain long-term server state between invocations.

- **Automatic Scaling:** Cloud providers handle the scaling of resources based on the demand for functions, ensuring cost efficiency.

c. Benefits:

- **Cost-Efficiency:** With serverless, you only pay for the actual execution time of functions, reducing infrastructure costs.

- **Scalability:** Serverless platforms automatically scale functions to handle varying workloads.

- **Reduced Operational Overhead:** Cloud providers manage server provisioning, patching, and maintenance.

- **Rapid Development:** Developers can focus on writing

code rather than managing infrastructure.

d. Challenges:

- **Cold Starts:** Serverless functions may experience a slight delay, known as a "cold start," when they are invoked for the first time or after being idle.

- **Resource Limits:** Serverless platforms impose resource limits on functions, which can impact certain workloads.

- **Vendor Lock-In:** Serverless platforms often require code to be written in specific languages or use proprietary APIs, potentially leading to vendor lock-in.

3. Combining Microservices and Serverless:

Organizations often combine microservices and serverless computing to build highly scalable and cost-efficient applications. In this approach, microservices orchestrate serverless functions to handle specific tasks or components, benefiting from both the flexibility of microservices and the efficiency of serverless execution.

Conclusion:

Microservices and serverless computing have reshaped cloud computing architectures, offering innovative ways to build scalable, resilient, and cost-effective applications. While they bring numerous benefits, they also introduce new challenges that organizations must address to fully leverage these architectural paradigms. As cloud technology continues to evolve, the combination of microservices and serverless computing will play an increasingly significant role in shaping the future of cloud-native applications.

B. Containers and Orchestration (Kubernetes): Revolutionizing Cloud Deployments

Containers and orchestration, with Kubernetes at the forefront, have become fundamental building blocks in modern cloud computing architectures. They provide a means to package, distribute, and manage applications and their dependencies in a highly efficient and scalable manner. In this in-depth exploration, we delve into the concepts, benefits, and intricacies of containers and Kubernetes orchestration.

1. Containers:

a. Definition: Containers are lightweight, standalone, and executable packages that contain everything needed to run a piece of software, including the code, runtime, libraries, and system tools. They provide consistency and isolation, making it possible to run applications consistently across different environments.

b. Key Concepts:

- **Image:** A container image is a pre-packaged, immutable snapshot of a containerized application, ensuring reproducibility.

- **Containerization:** Containers share the host OS kernel but run in isolated user spaces, making them highly efficient and portable.

- **Docker:** Docker is one of the most popular containerization platforms, providing tools for building, distributing, and running containers.

c. Benefits:

- **Portability:** Containers can run consistently on various platforms, from development laptops to production servers and cloud environments.

- **Efficiency:** Containers are lightweight and start quickly, making them ideal for microservices architectures and scaling applications.

- **Isolation:** Containers offer process and file system isolation, allowing multiple applications to run on the same host without interfering with each other.

d. Challenges:

- **Security:** Containers should be configured securely to prevent unauthorized access or privilege escalation.

- **Orchestration:** Manually managing containers at scale can be complex and challenging.

- **Networking:** Container networking requires careful configuration for communication between containers and with external resources.

2. Kubernetes:

a. Definition: Kubernetes, often abbreviated as K8s, is an open-source container orchestration platform originally developed by Google. It automates the deployment, scaling, and management of containerized applications, providing a powerful framework for managing container clusters.

b. Key Concepts:

- **Pod:** The smallest deployable unit in Kubernetes, a pod can contain one or more containers that share the same network and storage resources.

- **Replication Controller:** Ensures a specified number of pod replicas are running, making it possible to scale applications.

- **Service:** A Kubernetes service provides a stable network endpoint to connect to a set of pods, enabling load balancing and service discovery.

- **Ingress:** Manages external access to services, allowing for routing and SSL termination.

c. Benefits:

- **Scalability:** Kubernetes can automatically scale applications up or down based on defined criteria.

- **High Availability:** Kubernetes provides automated failover and load balancing to ensure applications remain available.

- **Declarative Configuration:** Infrastructure and application configurations are described in YAML files, enabling version control and reproducibility.

- **Ecosystem:** Kubernetes has a rich ecosystem of tools and extensions for monitoring, logging, and deploying applications.

d. Challenges:

- **Complexity:** Kubernetes has a steep learning curve and can be complex to configure and manage, especially for smaller-scale deployments.

- **Resource Requirements:** Running Kubernetes clusters requires sufficient resources, both in terms of hardware and operational overhead.

3. Combining Containers and Kubernetes:

Containers and Kubernetes are often used together to create a powerful and flexible platform for deploying and managing cloud-native applications. Kubernetes orchestrates containerized applications, scaling them as needed, while containers package and isolate the application components.

Conclusion:

Containers and Kubernetes orchestration have revolutionized how applications are deployed, managed, and scaled in cloud computing. They offer portability, scalability, and automation, making them essential technologies for organizations embracing cloud-native development and deployment practices. As the cloud landscape continues to evolve, containers and Kubernetes will remain integral to building and scaling modern applications efficiently and reliably.

C. DevOps and Continuous Integration/Continuous Deployment (CI/CD): Transforming Software Delivery

DevOps and CI/CD are two intertwined methodologies that

have revolutionized the software development and deployment processes. These practices emphasize collaboration, automation, and a continuous feedback loop, enabling organizations to accelerate software delivery, improve reliability, and respond rapidly to customer needs. In this in-depth exploration, we delve into the concepts, principles, benefits, and challenges of DevOps and CI/CD.

1. DevOps:

a. Definition: DevOps is a cultural and organizational approach that aims to bridge the gap between development (Dev) and IT operations (Ops). It promotes collaboration, communication, and automation to streamline the software delivery pipeline and improve the quality and reliability of applications.

b. Key Concepts:

- **Culture:** DevOps emphasizes a culture of collaboration, where development and operations teams work closely together, breaking down silos.

- **Automation:** Automation is a core tenet of DevOps, covering infrastructure provisioning, testing, and deployment processes.

- **Continuous Feedback:** DevOps encourages a

continuous feedback loop, with regular monitoring, measurement, and improvement of the software delivery pipeline.

c. Benefits:

- **Faster Delivery:** DevOps practices enable organizations to release software faster and more frequently, reducing time-to-market.

- **Improved Quality:** Automation of testing and deployment processes leads to higher software quality and reliability.

- **Efficiency:** DevOps automation reduces manual intervention, lowering operational costs and increasing efficiency.

d. Challenges:

- **Cultural Shift:** Implementing DevOps often requires a significant cultural shift within organizations, which can be met with resistance.

- **Tooling:** Selecting and implementing the right DevOps tools and technologies can be challenging.

2. Continuous Integration/Continuous Deployment (CI/CD):

a. Definition: CI/CD is a set of practices that automate the building, testing, and deployment of software changes.

Continuous Integration (CI) focuses on merging code changes into a shared repository and running automated tests. Continuous Deployment (CD) extends CI by automating the deployment of code to production environments.

b. Key Concepts:

- **Version Control:** CI/CD relies on version control systems (e.g., Git) to manage code changes and track revisions.

- **Automated Testing:** CI/CD pipelines include automated testing stages to ensure that code changes do not introduce defects.

- **Deployment Pipelines:** CD pipelines automate the deployment of code changes to production environments, often with multiple stages for testing and verification.

c. Benefits:

- **Rapid Feedback:** CI/CD provides rapid feedback to developers, allowing them to identify and fix issues early in the development process.

- **Reliability:** Automated testing and deployment reduce the likelihood of human errors and improve the reliability of deployments.

- **Consistency:** CI/CD pipelines ensure that code

changes are deployed consistently, eliminating configuration drift.

d. Challenges:

- **Complexity:** Implementing CI/CD pipelines can be complex, especially for large, legacy systems.
- **Security:** Ensuring the security of code changes and deployment processes is a challenge that requires careful consideration.

3. Combining DevOps and CI/CD:

DevOps and CI/CD are closely related and often used together. DevOps practices create a culture of collaboration and automation, while CI/CD pipelines automate the testing and deployment aspects of software delivery. Together, they enable organizations to achieve rapid, reliable, and frequent software releases.

Conclusion:

DevOps and CI/CD are transformative methodologies that have become essential for modern software development and deployment. They empower organizations to deliver software faster, with higher quality and reliability, while fostering collaboration and automation. As software development practices continue to evolve, the adoption of DevOps and CI/CD will remain crucial for organizations seeking to stay competitive in the digital age.

D. Cloud-Native Applications: Unleashing Agility and Innovation in the Cloud Era

Cloud-native applications represent a transformative approach to software development and deployment, designed from the ground up to harness the capabilities of cloud computing. These applications are architected with a focus on scalability, resilience, and rapid delivery, empowering organizations to respond to market demands with unprecedented speed and efficiency. In this in-depth exploration, we delve into the concepts, principles, benefits, and challenges of cloud-native applications.

1. Cloud-Native Application Fundamentals:

a. Definition: Cloud-native applications are designed to leverage cloud infrastructure and services, emphasizing characteristics such as microservices, containerization, serverless computing, and continuous delivery. They are optimized for scalability, resilience, and efficient resource utilization.

b. Key Concepts:

- **Microservices Architecture:** Cloud-native applications break down functionality into small, independent microservices that can be developed, deployed, and scaled independently.

- **Containers:** Containers are a fundamental building block of cloud-native applications, providing lightweight, isolated runtime environments for microservices.

- **Serverless Computing:** Serverless architectures allow developers to focus solely on writing code (functions) without managing underlying infrastructure.

c. Benefits:

- **Scalability:** Cloud-native applications can scale rapidly to accommodate varying workloads, ensuring optimal resource utilization.

- **Resilience:** Built-in redundancy and failover mechanisms enhance application resilience, minimizing downtime and data loss.

- **Rapid Deployment:** Continuous integration and continuous deployment (CI/CD) pipelines enable frequent and automated software releases.

d. Challenges:

- **Complexity:** Cloud-native applications can be complex to design, develop, and manage, requiring expertise in various technologies.

- **Cultural Shift:** Adopting a cloud-native approach

often necessitates cultural shifts within organizations, emphasizing collaboration, automation, and agility.

2. Core Principles of Cloud-Native Applications:

a. Automation:

- **Infrastructure as Code (IaC):** Cloud-native applications use IaC to automate the provisioning and configuration of infrastructure resources.

- **CI/CD Pipelines:** Automation is central to CI/CD pipelines, which streamline the testing and deployment of code changes.

b. Resilience:

- **Redundancy:** Cloud-native applications often incorporate redundancy, ensuring that system failures do not result in service outages.

- **Self-Healing:** Automation and monitoring enable self-healing mechanisms, where systems automatically recover from failures.

c. Observability:

- **Monitoring:** Real-time monitoring of application and infrastructure performance is critical for identifying and resolving issues promptly.

- **Logging:** Detailed logs provide visibility into application behavior and facilitate debugging.

d. Security:

- **Zero Trust Security:** Cloud-native applications often follow the zero trust security model, which assumes that threats may exist both inside and outside the network.

- **Identity and Access Management (IAM):** Robust IAM controls limit access to resources, reducing the attack surface.

3. Cloud-Native Ecosystem:

The cloud-native ecosystem comprises a rich set of tools and technologies, including Kubernetes for container orchestration, Docker for containerization, Istio for service mesh, and Prometheus for monitoring, among many others. These tools enable organizations to build, deploy, and manage cloud-native applications effectively.

Conclusion:

Cloud-native applications are at the forefront of modern software development, enabling organizations to respond to market demands with unprecedented speed and agility. By embracing cloud-native principles, organizations can build applications that are highly scalable, resilient, and efficient, ultimately delivering superior value to their customers in the cloud era. While adopting a cloud-native approach may present challenges, the rewards in terms of innovation, efficiency, and competitiveness are substantial.

CHAPTER 7

Cloud Storage and Databases

Cloud storage and databases are the dynamic duo of modern data management, providing organizations with flexible, scalable, and resilient solutions for storing, retrieving, and managing data in the cloud. In this introductory exploration, we embark on a journey into the realm of cloud storage and databases, where the cloud's infinite possibilities meet the needs of data-driven businesses, ushering in an era of innovation and efficiency in data management.

A. Cloud Storage Services: Redefining Data Management in the Digital Age

Cloud storage services have revolutionized the way organizations store, manage, and access their data. These services provide scalable and cost-effective solutions for storing vast amounts of information, offering reliability, security, and accessibility. In this in-depth exploration, we delve into the concepts, features, benefits, and challenges of cloud storage services.

1. Definition and Key Concepts:

a. Cloud Storage Services: Cloud storage services are third-party platforms that offer remote data storage on scalable infrastructure maintained by cloud providers. These services are accessible via the internet, allowing users to store and retrieve data from anywhere with an internet connection.

b. Key Concepts:

- **Data Redundancy:** Cloud storage services often replicate data across multiple data centers to ensure data availability and durability.

- **Scalability:** Users can scale their storage resources up or down as needed, paying only for the storage they use.

- **Data Types:** Cloud storage supports various data types, including structured (databases), semi-structured (documents), and unstructured (media files).

2. Types of Cloud Storage Services:

a. Object Storage:

- **Definition:** Object storage stores data as objects, including the data, metadata, and a unique identifier, in a flat namespace.

- **Use Cases:** Object storage is suitable for storing unstructured data such as images, videos, backups, and log files.

- **Examples:** Amazon S3, Google Cloud Storage, Azure Blob Storage.

b. File Storage:

- **Definition:** File storage organizes data into hierarchical file systems and allows multiple users or applications to access and modify files concurrently.

- **Use Cases:** File storage is ideal for shared documents, user home directories, and application data that requires shared access.

- **Examples:** Amazon EFS, Google Cloud Filestore, Azure Files.

c. Block Storage:

- **Definition:** Block storage divides data into fixed-sized blocks that are managed as individual units. It is often used to provide storage for virtual machines and databases.

- **Use Cases:** Block storage is suitable for databases, virtual machines, and applications requiring low-latency access to data.

- **Examples:** Amazon EBS, Google Persistent Disks, Azure Managed Disks.

3. Benefits of Cloud Storage Services:

a. Scalability:

- Cloud storage services offer virtually unlimited storage capacity, enabling organizations to scale their data storage needs seamlessly.

b. Cost-Efficiency:

- Pay-as-you-go pricing models mean organizations only pay for the storage they consume, reducing upfront capital expenditures.

c. Accessibility:

- Data stored in the cloud can be accessed from anywhere with an internet connection, facilitating remote work and global collaboration.

d. Data Redundancy and Durability:

- Cloud providers replicate data across multiple geographically dispersed data centers, ensuring high availability and data durability.

e. Security:

- Cloud storage services implement robust security measures, including encryption, access controls, and audit trails, to protect data.

4. Challenges:

a. Data Transfer Costs:

- Uploading or downloading large volumes of data to/from the cloud can incur data transfer fees, especially for organizations with limited bandwidth.

b. Data Privacy and Compliance:

- Ensuring compliance with data privacy regulations and industry standards can be complex when using cloud storage, especially for sensitive data.

c. Vendor Lock-In:

- Migrating data between cloud providers or back to on-premises infrastructure can be challenging due to proprietary formats and APIs.

d. Data Security Concerns:

- Organizations must implement proper security measures, including encryption and access controls, to protect data stored in the cloud.

Conclusion:

Cloud storage services have transformed data management,

offering scalable, cost-effective, and highly available solutions for organizations of all sizes. While they provide numerous benefits, organizations must carefully plan and implement their cloud storage strategies to address challenges and ensure data security, privacy, and compliance in the ever-evolving landscape of digital data management.

B. NoSQL and SQL Databases in the Cloud: Choosing the Right Database for Your Needs

Databases are the backbone of modern applications, and when it comes to cloud computing, organizations have a choice between SQL (Structured Query Language) and NoSQL (Not Only SQL) databases. Each type has its own strengths and use cases, and deploying them in the cloud offers scalability, flexibility, and cost-efficiency. In this in-depth exploration, we delve into the concepts, characteristics, benefits, and challenges of NoSQL and SQL databases in the cloud.

1. SQL Databases:

a. Definition: SQL databases are relational databases that use structured tables with rows and columns to store and manage data. They follow the principles of ACID (Atomicity, Consistency, Isolation, Durability) transactions and enforce a schema that defines the data's structure.

b. Key Concepts:

- **Tables:** SQL databases organize data into tables, where each row represents an entity, and each column represents an attribute.

- **Schema:** SQL databases enforce a schema that defines the structure, data types, and relationships between tables.

- **SQL Language:** SQL databases use a standardized query language (SQL) for data manipulation and retrieval.

c. Benefits:

- **Data Integrity:** SQL databases ensure data consistency and integrity through transactional support and referential integrity constraints.

- **ACID Compliance:** SQL databases guarantee that transactions are Atomic, Consistent, Isolated, and Durable, making them suitable for applications with complex data requirements.

- **Mature Ecosystem:** SQL databases have a mature ecosystem of tools, libraries, and expertise available.

d. Challenges:

- **Scaling:** Traditional SQL databases can be challenging to scale horizontally for high read/write workloads.

- **Schema Changes:** Modifying the schema of SQL databases can be complex and often requires careful planning.

2. NoSQL Databases:

a. Definition: NoSQL databases are non-relational databases designed to handle unstructured or semi-structured data. They are characterized by flexible schemas, horizontal scalability, and eventual consistency.

b. Key Concepts:

- **Document Stores:** NoSQL document databases store data in flexible, schema-less documents, often using JSON or BSON formats.

- **Key-Value Stores:** Key-value databases store data as pairs of keys and values, allowing for efficient retrieval.

- **Column-Family Stores:** Column-family databases organize data into column families, similar to tables but with dynamic schemas.

c. Benefits:

- **Scalability:** NoSQL databases are designed for horizontal scalability, making them well-suited for handling high volumes of data and traffic.

- **Flexibility:** The flexible schema of NoSQL databases

allows for agile development, accommodating evolving data structures.

- **High Availability:** Many NoSQL databases offer built-in high availability and fault tolerance features.

d. Challenges:

- **Lack of ACID Transactions:** NoSQL databases often prioritize availability and partition tolerance over strong consistency, leading to eventual consistency models.

- **Learning Curve:** NoSQL databases may require a learning curve for developers accustomed to relational databases.

3. Deploying Databases in the Cloud:

a. Cloud SQL Services: Cloud providers offer managed SQL database services (e.g., Amazon RDS, Azure SQL Database, Google Cloud SQL) that simplify database management, scaling, and backups.

b. NoSQL Database Services: Cloud platforms also provide managed NoSQL database services (e.g., Amazon DynamoDB, Azure Cosmos DB, Google Cloud Firestore) with automatic scaling and replication.

c. Benefits of Cloud Deployment: Cloud deployment of databases offers benefits like automated backups, scalability, disaster recovery, and cost optimization through pay-as-you-go pricing models.

Conclusion:

Choosing between NoSQL and SQL databases in the cloud depends on an organization's specific use cases, data requirements, and scalability needs. While SQL databases excel at ensuring data integrity and consistency, NoSQL databases offer flexibility and horizontal scalability. The decision ultimately depends on the trade-offs that best align with an organization's application goals, data structure, and performance demands in the cloud computing landscape.

C. Data Warehousing and Analytics in the Cloud: Unleashing the Power of Data

Data warehousing and analytics have become indispensable components of modern business intelligence and decision-making processes. In the cloud, these capabilities are elevated to new heights, offering organizations scalable, cost-effective, and high-performance solutions for storing, processing, and extracting insights from vast volumes of data. In this in-depth exploration, we delve into the concepts, principles, benefits, and challenges of data warehousing and analytics in the cloud.

1. Data Warehousing:

a. Definition: Data warehousing is the process of collecting, storing, and managing data from various sources in a central repository, known as a data warehouse. This repository is designed for efficient querying, reporting, and analysis.

b. Key Concepts:

- **ETL (Extract, Transform, Load):** Data warehousing involves extracting data from source systems, transforming it into a structured format, and loading it into the data warehouse.

- **Star and Snowflake Schemas:** Data warehouses often use star or snowflake schemas to organize data for efficient querying.

c. Benefits:

- **Centralized Data:** Data warehousing provides a single source of truth, ensuring that all stakeholders access consistent and up-to-date information.

- **Query Performance:** Data warehouses are optimized for querying and reporting, enabling fast and complex analytical queries.

- **Historical Data:** Data warehousing allows organizations to store historical data for trend analysis and compliance purposes.

d. Challenges:

- **Data Integration:** Integrating data from diverse sources can be complex and time-consuming.

- **Scalability:** Traditional data warehousing solutions may face limitations in scaling to handle massive datasets.

2. Cloud-Based Data Warehousing:

a. Cloud Data Warehouses: Cloud providers offer managed data warehousing services (e.g., Amazon Redshift, Google BigQuery, Azure Synapse Analytics) that eliminate the need for organizations to manage infrastructure, backups, and updates.

b. Benefits of Cloud Data Warehousing:

- **Scalability:** Cloud data warehouses can easily scale to accommodate growing data volumes and user loads.

- **Cost-Efficiency:** Organizations pay for the resources they consume, reducing upfront costs and minimizing operational overhead.

- **Managed Services:** Cloud providers handle routine maintenance tasks, allowing organizations to focus on data analysis.

c. Data Lake Integration: Many organizations combine data warehousing with data lakes in the cloud to store both structured and unstructured data, enabling advanced analytics and machine learning.

3. Analytics:

a. Definition: Analytics involves the exploration and interpretation of data to gain insights, make informed decisions, and drive business improvements.

b. Types of Analytics:

- **Descriptive Analytics:** Descriptive analytics provides an overview of historical data, offering insights into past performance and trends.

- **Predictive Analytics:** Predictive analytics uses historical data to build models that forecast future outcomes or trends.

- **Prescriptive Analytics:** Prescriptive analytics goes beyond predictions, recommending actions to optimize outcomes.

c. Tools and Technologies: Cloud-based analytics platforms (e.g., AWS SageMaker, Google AI Platform, Azure Machine Learning) provide machine learning and analytics capabilities in a scalable and accessible manner.

4. Benefits and Challenges:

a. Benefits of Cloud-Based Analytics:

- **Scalability:** Cloud-based analytics platforms offer the computational power needed for complex modeling and analysis tasks.

- **Accessibility:** Cloud-based analytics tools are accessible from anywhere with an internet connection, promoting collaboration and remote work.

- **Cost-Efficiency:** Organizations can scale resources up or down based on demand, optimizing costs.

b. Challenges:

- **Data Quality:** Data quality is essential for accurate analytics, and ensuring data cleanliness can be challenging.

- **Data Privacy and Security:** Protecting sensitive data and complying with regulations is a top concern in cloud-based analytics.

Conclusion:

Data warehousing and analytics in the cloud empower organizations to harness the full potential of their data, enabling data-driven decision-making and uncovering valuable insights. The scalability, cost-efficiency, and accessibility of cloud-based solutions make them an ideal choice for businesses looking to leverage their data for competitive advantage in the digital age. However, organizations must also address data integration, quality, privacy, and security challenges to fully realize the benefits of cloud-based data warehousing and analytics.

D. Data Migration and Backup Strategies in the Cloud: Ensuring Data Resilience and Accessibility

Data migration and backup are critical aspects of data management, ensuring the availability, integrity, and security of data in the cloud. In the cloud environment, where data is dispersed across distributed resources, effective strategies for moving, replicating, and safeguarding data are essential. In this in-depth exploration, we delve into the concepts, principles, benefits, and challenges of data migration and backup strategies in the cloud.

1. Data Migration:

a. Definition: Data migration is the process of moving data from one location, format, or system to another. In the context of cloud computing, it involves transferring data from on-premises environments, other cloud providers, or between cloud services.

b. Key Concepts:

- **ETL (Extract, Transform, Load):** Data migration often follows an ETL process, which involves extracting data from the source, transforming it as necessary, and loading it into the target system.

- **Data Synchronization:** In some cases, data migration requires ongoing synchronization between the source and target to ensure data consistency during the transition.

c. Benefits:

- **Scalability:** Cloud-based data migration tools and services can scale to handle large volumes of data, making them suitable for big data and data warehousing projects.

- **Reduced Downtime:** Effective data migration strategies aim to minimize downtime during the transition, ensuring business continuity.

d. Challenges:

- **Data Consistency:** Maintaining data consistency between source and target systems, especially during ongoing migrations, can be complex.

- **Data Validation:** Ensuring that data is migrated accurately and without corruption is crucial for data integrity.

2. Data Backup:

a. Definition: Data backup involves creating copies of data to protect against data loss, corruption, or disasters. In the cloud, backup strategies can include regular backups, versioning, and redundancy.

b. Key Concepts:

- **Backup Types:** Cloud providers often offer various backup types, including full backups, incremental backups, and snapshot backups.

- **Versioning:** Many cloud storage services support versioning, which enables users to access previous versions of data.

c. Benefits:

- **Data Resilience:** Regular backups ensure data resilience, allowing organizations to recover from data loss or disasters.

- **Data Recovery:** Backups provide a safety net for data recovery in cases of accidental deletion, malware attacks, or hardware failures.

d. Challenges:

- **Cost Management:** Storing backups in the cloud can

incur storage costs, and organizations must balance data retention needs with budget constraints.

- **Data Security:** Safeguarding backups is essential to prevent unauthorized access or data breaches.

3. Data Migration and Backup Strategies in the Cloud:

a. Cloud-Based Data Migration Tools: Cloud providers offer migration services and tools (e.g., AWS DataSync, Azure Data Factory) that simplify data migration tasks.

b. Backup and Disaster Recovery Services: Cloud platforms provide managed backup and disaster recovery services (e.g., AWS Backup, Google Cloud Backup, Azure Backup) that automate backup processes and ensure data recoverability.

c. Data Lifecycle Policies: Organizations can implement data lifecycle policies that automate data migration and archiving based on defined criteria, optimizing storage costs.

d. Redundancy and Replication: Cloud providers often replicate data across multiple data centers or regions, enhancing data redundancy and availability.

4. Compliance and Data Governance:

Organizations must consider compliance requirements and data governance when developing data migration and backup strategies, especially when handling sensitive or regulated data. Compliance standards, such as GDPR, HIPAA, and industry-specific regulations, may dictate specific data retention and protection practices.

Conclusion:

Effective data migration and backup strategies in the cloud are essential for ensuring data resilience, accessibility, and compliance. Cloud-based tools and services offer scalability and automation, simplifying these tasks. However, organizations must carefully plan and execute their strategies to address data consistency, validation, cost management, and security challenges in the ever-evolving landscape of cloud computing.

CHAPTER 8

Cloud Cost Management

Cloud cost management is a crucial discipline in the era of cloud computing, where organizations leverage cloud services to scale and innovate. While the cloud offers flexibility and efficiency, it also brings the challenge of controlling costs effectively. In this introductory exploration, we embark on a journey into the realm of cloud cost management, where we unravel the strategies, tools, and best practices for optimizing your cloud investment and ensuring cost-effectiveness in the cloud era.

A. Cost Structures in the Cloud: Navigating the Economics of Cloud Computing

Understanding the cost structures in the cloud is fundamental to effective cloud cost management. Cloud providers offer a variety of pricing models and billing mechanisms, each with its own nuances. In this in-depth exploration, we delve into the key cost structures in the cloud, shedding light on the complexities, advantages, and considerations associated with cloud computing economics.

1. Pay-as-You-Go (PAYG):

a. Definition: Pay-as-you-go is the most prevalent pricing model in the cloud. It charges users based on their actual usage of cloud resources, typically by the hour or second. Users pay for what they consume, with no upfront commitments.

b. Advantages:

- **Flexibility:** PAYG offers the flexibility to scale resources up or down as needed, aligning costs with demand.
- **Cost-Efficiency:** Small and medium-sized enterprises benefit from PAYG, as they can access advanced resources without high initial costs.

c. Considerations:

- **Cost Monitoring:** Frequent monitoring of resource usage is essential to prevent unexpected cost overruns.
- **Resource Optimization:** Organizations should continuously optimize resource usage to avoid unnecessary costs.

2. Reserved Instances (RIs):

a. Definition: Reserved Instances allow users to commit to a specific amount of cloud capacity for a fixed period, typically one or three years. In return, they receive a significant discount compared to PAYG rates.

b. Advantages:

- **Cost Savings:** RIs can result in substantial cost savings, especially for predictable workloads.

- **Capacity Assurance:** Organizations can secure capacity for mission-critical applications.

c. Considerations:

- **Upfront Payment:** RIs require an upfront payment, which can be a barrier for some organizations.

- **Limited Flexibility:** RIs are less flexible than PAYG and may lead to underutilization if not correctly matched with workloads.

3. Spot Instances:

a. Definition: Spot Instances allow users to bid for unused cloud capacity at significantly reduced prices compared to PAYG rates. However, they can be terminated if the capacity is needed by another user.

b. Advantages:

- **Cost Savings:** Spot Instances offer the lowest cost but require flexibility in workload scheduling.

- **Batch Processing:** They are ideal for batch

processing, data analysis, and workloads that can be interrupted without impact.

c. Considerations:

- **Termination Risk:** Spot Instances may be terminated with little notice when capacity is needed elsewhere.
- **Unpredictability:** Organizations must design workloads to handle interruptions and resumptions.

4. Cost Management Tools:

Cloud providers offer cost management tools (e.g., AWS Cost Explorer, Azure Cost Management, Google Cloud Cost Management) to track and analyze spending, identify cost-saving opportunities, and set budgets and alerts.

5. Conclusion:

Effectively managing cloud costs requires a deep understanding of the available cost structures and the ability to align them with an organization's specific needs and workloads. By leveraging the right mix of PAYG, RIs, Spot Instances, and cost management tools, organizations can strike a balance between cost optimization and resource flexibility in the cloud. Ultimately, mastering cloud cost management is an ongoing process, enabling organizations to maximize the value of their cloud investments while controlling expenditure.

B. Cost Monitoring and Optimization Tools in the Cloud: Navigating the Path to Efficient Cloud Spending

Cost monitoring and optimization tools are indispensable components of cloud cost management. In the dynamic world of cloud computing, where resources can be provisioned and de-provisioned at a click, maintaining control over costs is paramount. In this in-depth exploration, we delve into the significance, features, benefits, and challenges of cost monitoring and optimization tools in the cloud.

1. The Importance of Cost Monitoring and Optimization:

a. Cost Visibility: Cloud environments generate vast amounts of cost-related data. Cost monitoring tools provide visibility into this data, helping organizations understand where their cloud spending is going.

b. Resource Efficiency: Cost optimization tools identify underutilized resources, allowing organizations to rightsize or decommission them, thereby reducing costs.

c. Budget Control: With budgets and alerts, organizations can set spending limits and receive notifications when costs approach or exceed these limits.

2. Key Features of Cost Monitoring and Optimization Tools:

a. Cost Visualization:

- **Dashboard:** Tools often provide a dashboard displaying an overview of current and historical costs.

- **Reports:** Detailed cost reports allow organizations to drill down into spending by resource, service, or user.

b. Resource Recommendations:

- **Idle Resource Detection:** Tools identify resources that are underutilized or idle and suggest actions, such as resizing or termination.

- **Rightsizing:** Recommendations may include changing instance types or adjusting storage sizes for optimal cost efficiency.

c. Budgeting and Alerts:

- **Budget Setting:** Organizations can set budgets based on spending thresholds, user accounts, or services.

- **Alerts:** Notifications are triggered when actual spending approaches or exceeds budgeted amounts.

d. Cost Allocation:

- **Tagging:** Tools support resource tagging, allowing organizations to allocate costs to specific projects, departments, or teams.

- **Showback/Chargeback:** Cost allocation enables organizations to show or charge costs back to respective stakeholders.

e. Anomaly Detection:

- **Anomaly Identification:** Some tools use machine learning to detect unusual cost patterns or spikes, which could indicate potential issues or optimization opportunities.

3. Benefits of Cost Monitoring and Optimization Tools:

a. Cost Savings: By identifying and addressing inefficiencies, organizations can significantly reduce their cloud spending.

b. Cost Predictability: Budgeting and alerts help organizations maintain cost predictability and avoid unexpected overages.

c. Resource Efficiency: Right-sizing and decommissioning underutilized resources improve resource efficiency and reduce wastage.

4. Challenges and Considerations:

a. Tool Selection: There are numerous cost monitoring and optimization tools available, and organizations must choose one that aligns with their cloud provider and specific needs.

b. Data Complexity: Cloud cost data can be complex, making it challenging to interpret and act upon without the right toolset.

c. Ongoing Monitoring: Effective cost management is an ongoing process that requires continuous monitoring and optimization efforts.

d. Cost of Tools: While cost monitoring and optimization tools can yield significant savings, organizations must also consider the cost of these tools in their overall budget.

5. Cloud Provider Tools:

Most major cloud providers offer their native cost monitoring and optimization tools. For example, AWS provides AWS Cost Explorer and AWS Trusted Advisor, Google Cloud offers Google Cloud Cost Management, and Azure provides Azure Cost Management and Billing.

Conclusion:

Cost monitoring and optimization tools are essential for organizations seeking to maximize the value of their cloud investments while maintaining control over spending. These tools provide the visibility, recommendations, and budgeting capabilities necessary to achieve efficient cloud cost management. By proactively monitoring, analyzing, and optimizing cloud costs, organizations can harness the full potential of cloud computing while keeping expenditures in check.

C. Budgeting and Forecasting in the Cloud: Ensuring Financial Control and Planning

Budgeting and forecasting are critical components of cloud cost management, helping organizations control spending and plan for future cloud expenditures. In the dynamic world of cloud computing, where resources are provisioned and scaled with ease, having a well-defined budget and accurate forecasts is essential for financial stability. In this in-depth exploration, we delve into the significance, processes, benefits, and challenges of budgeting and forecasting in the cloud.

1. Significance of Budgeting and Forecasting:

a. Cost Control: Budgets set spending limits and provide a framework for monitoring and controlling cloud costs, preventing unexpected overruns.

b. Financial Planning: Forecasts allow organizations to plan for future cloud expenditures, aligning cloud resources with business objectives.

2. The Budgeting Process:

a. Establishing Budgets:

- **Baseline Budget:** Organizations create an initial budget based on historical spending and expected resource needs.

- **Resource Allocation:** Budgets allocate funds to specific cloud services, projects, or teams.

b. Monitoring and Adjusting:

- **Regular Review:** Budgets are monitored regularly to track actual spending against the budgeted amounts.

- **Adjustments:** If actual spending deviates significantly from the budget, adjustments may be necessary.

c. Cloud Cost Categories:

- **Fixed Costs:** Costs that remain constant, such as reserved instances.

- **Variable Costs:** Costs that fluctuate with usage, like pay-as-you-go resources.

- **One-time Costs:** Non-recurring expenses, such as setup or migration costs.

3. The Forecasting Process:

a. Data Analysis:

- **Historical Data:** Organizations analyze historical cost data to identify trends and patterns.

- **Growth Projections:** Forecasts consider expected business growth and resource demand.

b. Modeling and Prediction:

- **Scenario Modeling:** Organizations create different scenarios based on various assumptions to predict future costs.

- **Machine Learning:** Some organizations use machine learning algorithms to improve forecasting accuracy.

c. Time Horizons:

- **Short-Term:** Short-term forecasts typically cover the next few months and are used for immediate planning.

- **Long-Term:** Long-term forecasts span years and guide strategic planning.

4. Benefits of Budgeting and Forecasting:

a. Cost Visibility: Budgets provide a clear view of expected spending, helping organizations allocate resources wisely.

b. Financial Discipline: Budgets enforce financial discipline and prevent overspending.

c. Resource Optimization: Forecasts enable organizations to allocate resources efficiently, avoiding under-provisioning or over-provisioning.

d. Strategic Planning: Long-term forecasts support strategic planning by aligning cloud spending with business goals.

5. Challenges and Considerations:

a. Data Accuracy: Accurate forecasts require clean and reliable historical data.

b. Cloud Cost Complexity: Cloud billing models and services can be complex, making it challenging to accurately predict costs.

c. Cloud Cost Variability: Costs can fluctuate due to factors like seasonal demand or unexpected usage spikes.

d. Tool Selection: Choosing the right budgeting and forecasting tools or software is critical for success.

e. Communication: Effective communication and collaboration between finance, IT, and cloud teams are essential for accurate forecasts and budget adherence.

6. Cloud-Native Budgeting and Forecasting Tools:

Many cloud providers offer cloud-native tools and services to assist with budgeting and forecasting. For example, AWS provides AWS Budgets, Google Cloud offers Google Cloud Cost Management, and Azure provides Azure Cost Management and Billing.

Conclusion:

Budgeting and forecasting in the cloud are essential practices that help organizations maintain control over spending, plan for the future, and align cloud resources with business goals. By implementing robust budgeting and forecasting processes, organizations can optimize resource allocation, enhance financial discipline, and make informed decisions in the dynamic and ever-evolving landscape of cloud computing.

D. Strategies for Cost Reduction in the Cloud: Maximizing Efficiency and Value

Cost reduction in the cloud is a paramount concern for organizations seeking to optimize their cloud investments. While cloud computing offers scalability and flexibility, it can also lead to unexpected expenses if not managed efficiently. In this in-depth exploration, we delve into the essential strategies and best practices for reducing costs in the cloud environment.

1. Rightsizing Resources:

a. Rightsize Instances: Matching cloud instances to actual workload requirements is crucial. Overprovisioning can lead to wasted resources, while underprovisioning may result in performance issues. Continuous monitoring and adjustment of instance types can help achieve the right balance.

b. Autoscaling: Implement autoscaling policies to dynamically adjust resources based on workload demands. Autoscaling ensures that you're not paying for idle resources during periods of low activity.

2. Reserved Instances (RIs) and Savings Plans:

a. Utilize RIs: Reserved Instances provide significant cost savings compared to pay-as-you-go pricing. Committing to long-term RIs can lead to substantial discounts, especially for stable workloads.

b. Savings Plans: Savings Plans offer flexibility across different instance types and families, providing savings for variable workloads. They are an alternative to traditional RIs.

3. Spot Instances and Preemptible VMs:

a. Leverage Spot Instances: Spot Instances (AWS) and Preemptible VMs (Google Cloud) offer steep discounts for workloads that can tolerate interruptions. They are ideal for batch processing, rendering, and other non-critical tasks.

b. Checkpointing: For workloads using Spot Instances or Preemptible VMs, implement checkpointing to ensure that progress is saved and can be resumed if instances are interrupted.

4. Cloud Storage Optimization:

a. Data Lifecycle Policies: Implement data lifecycle policies to move less frequently accessed data to lower-cost storage tiers, such as Amazon S3 Glacier or Azure Cool Blob Storage.

b. Deduplication and Compression: Use deduplication and compression techniques to reduce storage costs while maintaining data integrity.

5. Containerization and Serverless Computing:

a. Container Orchestration: Adopt container orchestration platforms like Kubernetes to efficiently manage and scale containerized workloads, ensuring optimal resource utilization.

b. Serverless Functions: Use serverless computing to pay only for the compute resources consumed during the execution of functions, eliminating the need for managing server instances.

6. Cost Monitoring and Optimization Tools:

a. Native Tools: Leverage cloud providers' cost monitoring and optimization tools, such as AWS Cost Explorer, Azure Cost

Management, and Google Cloud Cost Management, to gain insights into spending patterns and identify optimization opportunities.

b. Third-Party Tools: Consider using third-party cost management solutions that offer advanced analytics and optimization recommendations.

7. Data Transfer and Network Costs:

a. Data Transfer Planning: Minimize data transfer costs by strategically placing resources in the same region or availability zone.

b. Content Delivery Networks (CDNs): Implement CDNs to cache and serve content closer to end-users, reducing data transfer costs and improving latency.

8. Periodic Review and Optimization:

a. Regular Review: Continuously monitor and review your cloud infrastructure for cost optimization opportunities. Cloud environments are dynamic, and optimization needs can change over time.

b. Cloud Cost Optimization Teams: Establish cross-functional teams responsible for cost optimization efforts, including finance, IT, and cloud operations.

9. Cost Governance and Policies:

a. Cost Allocation: Implement cost allocation and tagging policies to assign costs to specific projects, departments, or teams, facilitating showback or chargeback.

b. Cost Budgets: Set and enforce cost budgets for different areas of your organization, promoting financial discipline.

10. Training and Education:

Invest in cloud cost management training and education for your teams to ensure that best practices are followed and that everyone understands the impact of their choices on costs.

Conclusion:

Cost reduction in the cloud is an ongoing process that requires vigilance, optimization efforts, and a keen understanding of your cloud environment. By implementing these strategies and best practices, organizations can maximize the efficiency and value of their cloud investments, achieving the right balance between resource availability and cost control in the ever-evolving landscape of cloud computing.

CHAPTER 9

Cloud Governance and Compliance

Cloud governance and compliance are paramount in today's digital landscape, where organizations increasingly rely on cloud services to drive innovation and growth. Effective governance and compliance frameworks are essential to maintain control, security, and adherence to regulatory standards in cloud environments. In this introductory exploration, we embark on a journey into the world of cloud governance and compliance, where we unravel the strategies, principles, and best practices for navigating this complex and critical domain of cloud computing.

A. Governance Frameworks in the Cloud: Navigating the Landscape of Control and Compliance

In the realm of cloud computing, governance frameworks serve as essential guidelines and structures for organizations to ensure control, security, and compliance. These frameworks provide a systematic approach to managing cloud resources, mitigating risks, and adhering to regulatory standards. In this in-depth exploration, we delve into the significance, components, and implementation strategies of governance frameworks in the cloud.

1. Significance of Governance Frameworks:

a. Control and Accountability: Governance frameworks establish clear lines of control, responsibility, and accountability within cloud environments, ensuring that resources are used in a controlled and efficient manner.

b. Risk Mitigation: Effective governance helps identify, assess, and mitigate risks associated with cloud usage, reducing the potential impact of security breaches, data loss, and compliance violations.

c. Compliance Adherence: Governance frameworks provide a structured approach to aligning cloud practices with regulatory requirements, industry standards, and internal policies.

2. Components of Governance Frameworks:

a. Policies and Procedures:

- **Cloud Usage Policies:** Define the acceptable use of cloud resources, including data handling, access controls, and resource provisioning.

- **Incident Response Procedures:** Establish guidelines for addressing security incidents, breaches, and data breaches.

b. Roles and Responsibilities:

- **Cloud Governance Teams:** Define teams responsible

for cloud governance, including roles such as cloud architects, security officers, and compliance managers.

- **Accountability:** Clearly assign responsibilities for various aspects of cloud management, from access control to cost monitoring.

c. Standards and Best Practices:

- **Security Standards:** Establish security standards that address data encryption, access control, identity management, and threat detection.

- **Compliance Frameworks:** Align with industry-specific compliance frameworks (e.g., HIPAA, GDPR) and implement controls to meet these standards.

d. Monitoring and Reporting:

- **Continuous Monitoring:** Implement tools and processes for monitoring cloud resources, security incidents, and compliance violations in real-time.

- **Reporting:** Create mechanisms for generating compliance reports, cost analysis reports, and security incident reports.

e. Automation and Orchestration:

- **Automation:** Leverage automation tools to enforce

policies, manage resources, and respond to incidents efficiently.

- **Orchestration:** Orchestration frameworks enable seamless integration of cloud services and resources while ensuring governance and compliance requirements are met.

3. Implementation Strategies:

a. Assess Your Cloud Environment:

- **Inventory:** Create an inventory of all cloud resources, including virtual machines, databases, storage, and network configurations.

- **Risk Assessment:** Perform a risk assessment to identify vulnerabilities and compliance gaps.

b. Develop and Document Policies:

- **Cloud Usage Policies:** Draft clear and comprehensive cloud usage policies, including data handling, access controls, and resource allocation.

- **Incident Response Plans:** Develop incident response plans that outline the steps to take in the event of security incidents or breaches.

c. Training and Education:

- **Employee Training:** Provide training and education

to employees and teams involved in cloud operations to ensure they understand and adhere to governance policies.

d. Implement Monitoring and Reporting:

- **Monitoring Tools:** Deploy cloud monitoring tools and security solutions to continuously monitor cloud resources and detect anomalies.

- **Reporting Mechanisms:** Establish reporting mechanisms to generate compliance reports and incident reports.

e. Automation and Orchestration:

- **Policy Enforcement:** Utilize automation and orchestration to enforce policies, such as automatically encrypting data or scaling resources based on demand.

- **Incident Response Automation:** Automate incident response processes to reduce the time and impact of security incidents.

4. Compliance Auditing and Assessment:

a. Regular Auditing: Conduct regular compliance audits to ensure that cloud practices align with governance frameworks and regulatory requirements.

b. Assessment: Continuously assess the effectiveness of governance controls and make adjustments as needed based on audit findings.

Conclusion:

Governance frameworks in the cloud are indispensable for organizations looking to maintain control, security, and compliance in their cloud environments. By implementing comprehensive governance frameworks, organizations can align their cloud practices with industry standards, regulatory requirements, and internal policies, while mitigating risks and ensuring efficient resource management in the dynamic landscape of cloud computing.

B. Compliance Requirements in the Cloud: Navigating GDPR, HIPAA, and Beyond

Compliance with regulatory requirements is a critical aspect of cloud governance, especially when handling sensitive data and personal information. Two prominent regulatory frameworks, GDPR (General Data Protection Regulation) and HIPAA (Health Insurance Portability and Accountability Act), set stringent standards for data protection and privacy. In this in-depth exploration, we delve into the significance, key components, and strategies for achieving compliance with these regulations in the cloud.

1. GDPR (General Data Protection Regulation):

a. Significance of GDPR Compliance:

- **Data Protection:** GDPR aims to protect the privacy and personal data of individuals within the European Union (EU). Compliance is vital for organizations that handle EU residents' data, even if the organization is based outside the EU.

- **Penalties:** Non-compliance with GDPR can result in significant fines, which can amount to millions of euros or a percentage of global annual turnover, depending on the severity of the violation.

b. Key Components of GDPR Compliance:

i. Data Processing Principles:

- **Lawfulness, Fairness, and Transparency:** Organizations must process personal data legally and transparently, with clear consent from individuals.

- **Purpose Limitation:** Data must be collected and processed for specific, legitimate purposes and not used for unrelated activities.

- **Data Minimization:** Collect and retain only the data necessary for the intended purpose.

ii. Data Subject Rights:

- **Right to Access:** Individuals can request access to their personal data held by organizations.

- **Right to Erasure (Right to be Forgotten):** Individuals can request the deletion of their data under certain circumstances.

- **Data Portability:** Data subjects have the right to receive their data in a machine-readable format.

iii. Data Security:

- **Data Protection Impact Assessments (DPIAs):** Organizations must conduct DPIAs to assess and mitigate risks to data subjects' rights and freedoms.

- **Data Breach Notification:** GDPR mandates prompt reporting of data breaches to data protection authorities and affected individuals.

iv. Data Protection Officers (DPOs):

- Organizations may need to appoint a DPO responsible for ensuring GDPR compliance and acting as a point of contact for data protection authorities.

2. HIPAA (Health Insurance Portability and Accountability Act):

a. Significance of HIPAA Compliance:

- **Healthcare Data Protection:** HIPAA applies to healthcare organizations and their business associates in the United States. It sets strict standards for safeguarding protected health information (PHI).

- **Penalties:** Non-compliance with HIPAA can result in severe penalties, including fines and legal actions.

b. Key Components of HIPAA Compliance:

i. Administrative Safeguards:

- **Policies and Procedures:** Develop and implement policies and procedures for compliance.

- **Security Officer:** Appoint a security officer responsible for overseeing security policies and procedures.

ii. Physical Safeguards:

- **Access Controls:** Implement physical access controls to protect PHI stored in physical formats.

- **Facility Security:** Secure facilities housing PHI to prevent unauthorized access.

iii. Technical Safeguards:

- **Access Controls:** Implement access controls, including user authentication and authorization, to protect electronic PHI (ePHI).

- **Data Encryption:** Encrypt ePHI to protect it during storage and transmission.

iv. Breach Notification:

- HIPAA requires organizations to report breaches of unsecured PHI to affected individuals, the U.S. Department of Health and Human Services (HHS), and, in some cases, the media.

v. Business Associate Agreements (BAAs):

- Covered entities must have BAAs in place with vendors and service providers who handle PHI.

3. Achieving Compliance in the Cloud:

a. Data Encryption: Encrypt data at rest and in transit using strong encryption protocols and keys.

b. Access Control: Implement strict access controls and authentication mechanisms to ensure that only authorized personnel can access sensitive data.

c. Auditing and Logging: Maintain detailed logs of activities and events within the cloud environment to track data access and changes.

d. Data Residency: Ensure that data is stored in regions or data centers compliant with the regulations.

e. Vendor Assessment: Evaluate cloud service providers' security and compliance measures and ensure they provide tools and features to support compliance.

f. Training and Awareness: Train staff and raise awareness of the importance of compliance, including data protection and privacy practices.

Conclusion:

Compliance with GDPR, HIPAA, and other regulatory frameworks is essential for organizations that handle sensitive data. Achieving and maintaining compliance in the cloud requires a multifaceted approach, including robust security measures, strict access controls, vigilant monitoring, and ongoing training and awareness programs. By adhering to these standards, organizations can protect sensitive information, avoid penalties, and maintain trust with their customers and stakeholders.

C. Auditing and Monitoring in the Cloud: Ensuring Security and Compliance

Auditing and monitoring are essential components of cloud governance and security. In the dynamic and distributed landscape of cloud computing, organizations must continuously track and assess their cloud resources and activities to ensure security, compliance, and operational excellence. In this in-depth exploration, we delve into the significance, key components, and best practices for auditing and monitoring in the cloud.

1. Significance of Auditing and Monitoring:

a. Security Assurance:

- Auditing and monitoring provide real-time visibility into cloud environments, allowing organizations to detect and respond to security threats promptly.
- Continuous monitoring helps identify vulnerabilities, misconfigurations, and unauthorized access, bolstering security.

b. Compliance Adherence:

- Regulatory standards often require organizations to maintain audit trails and monitor activities to ensure compliance with data protection and privacy laws.

c. Operational Insights:

- Monitoring provides valuable insights into resource utilization, performance, and efficiency, helping organizations optimize cloud operations.

2. Key Components of Auditing and Monitoring:

a. Log Management:

- Collect logs from various cloud services and resources, including virtual machines, databases, storage, and networking components.

- Centralize log storage in a secure and accessible location.

b. Real-time Monitoring:

- Implement real-time monitoring tools and services to track activities and events as they occur.

- Define alerting thresholds for critical events or anomalies.

c. Configuration Management:

- Continuously assess and manage the configurations of cloud resources to ensure adherence to security best practices and compliance requirements.

d. Security Information and Event Management (SIEM):

- SIEM solutions aggregate and analyze log data from multiple sources, enabling correlation and alerting for security incidents.

e. Threat Detection and Incident Response:

- Employ threat detection mechanisms to identify suspicious or malicious activities.

- Develop incident response plans and playbooks for handling security incidents detected through monitoring.

f. Cloud-native Monitoring Services:

- Major cloud providers offer native monitoring services, such as AWS CloudWatch, Azure Monitor, and Google Cloud Monitoring, to track cloud-specific metrics and events.

g. Compliance Auditing Tools:

- Use compliance auditing tools and services to automate assessments against regulatory standards and best practices.

3. Best Practices for Auditing and Monitoring:

a. Define Monitoring Objectives:

- Clearly define the objectives of your auditing and

monitoring efforts, including security, compliance, and performance optimization.

b. Granular Logging:

- Enable granular logging for critical resources and services, capturing relevant events and activities.

c. Log Retention:

- Establish log retention policies to retain logs for an appropriate duration based on compliance and operational needs.

d. Continuous Assessment:

- Continuously assess cloud configurations to detect and remediate vulnerabilities and misconfigurations.

e. Automated Alerts:

- Set up automated alerts for critical events, ensuring timely response to security incidents or performance issues.

f. Incident Response Plan:

- Develop a well-defined incident response plan that outlines roles, responsibilities, and actions to take in the event of security incidents.

g. Periodic Audits:

- Conduct periodic compliance audits to ensure that cloud resources adhere to regulatory standards and internal policies.

h. Training and Awareness:

- Train staff on the importance of auditing and monitoring and ensure they are familiar with tools and procedures.

4. Cloud Provider Tools:

- Leverage cloud provider-specific monitoring and auditing tools to gain insights into cloud-native metrics and events.

5. Third-party Solutions:

- Consider third-party auditing and monitoring solutions for additional features, customization, and integration capabilities.

Conclusion:

Auditing and monitoring are indispensable practices in cloud computing, supporting security, compliance, and operational efficiency. By implementing robust auditing and monitoring strategies, organizations can proactively detect and respond to security threats, ensure compliance with regulatory standards, and optimize their cloud operations to achieve excellence in the dynamic and ever-evolving cloud environment.

D. Risk Management in the Cloud: Navigating the Evolving Landscape

Risk management in the cloud is a complex and ever-evolving process that involves identifying, assessing, mitigating, and monitoring risks associated with cloud adoption. As organizations increasingly rely on cloud services to drive innovation and efficiency, it is crucial to understand and effectively manage the risks that come with this transformative technology. In this in-depth exploration, we delve into the significance, key components, and best practices for risk management in the cloud.

1. Significance of Risk Management in the Cloud:

a. Risk Exposure:

- Cloud adoption introduces a variety of risks, including security breaches, data loss, compliance violations, and operational disruptions.

b. Regulatory and Legal Implications:

- Non-compliance with data protection and privacy regulations can result in severe legal and financial consequences.

c. Reputation and Trust:

- Security incidents and data breaches can damage an organization's reputation and erode customer trust.

2. Key Components of Risk Management in the Cloud:

a. Risk Identification:

- Identify and document potential risks associated with cloud adoption, considering factors such as data sensitivity, service dependencies, and threat landscape.

b. Risk Assessment:

- Assess the likelihood and potential impact of identified risks to prioritize mitigation efforts.

c. Risk Mitigation:

- Develop and implement risk mitigation strategies, which may include security measures, compliance controls, and disaster recovery plans.

d. Risk Monitoring:

- Continuously monitor cloud environments and activities to detect and respond to emerging risks and vulnerabilities.

e. Incident Response and Recovery:

- Establish incident response and recovery plans to manage and recover from security incidents and data breaches.

f. Compliance Management:

- Ensure that cloud operations align with relevant regulatory and compliance standards, such as GDPR, HIPAA, or industry-specific requirements.

3. Best Practices for Risk Management in the Cloud:

a. Security Controls:

- Implement robust security controls, including access management, encryption, intrusion detection, and vulnerability scanning.

b. Data Classification:

- Classify data based on its sensitivity and importance to prioritize security measures.

c. Regular Auditing:

- Conduct regular security audits and compliance assessments to ensure adherence to security policies and standards.

d. Incident Response Planning:

- Develop and regularly test incident response plans to reduce the impact of security incidents.

e. Data Backup and Recovery:

- Implement reliable data backup and recovery mechanisms to ensure business continuity.

f. Security Training:

- Provide security awareness and training programs to educate staff on security best practices.

g. Vendor Assessment:

- Assess the security and compliance practices of cloud service providers, ensuring they meet organizational standards.

h. Risk Awareness and Culture:

- Foster a culture of risk awareness and accountability throughout the organization.

4. Cloud Provider Responsibility vs. Shared Responsibility Model:

- Understand the shared responsibility model, which outlines the division of security responsibilities between the cloud provider and the customer.

5. Third-party Risk Management:

- Evaluate and manage risks associated with third-party vendors and service providers that interact with your cloud environment.

6. Continuous Improvement:

- Continuously review and update risk management strategies to adapt to changing threat landscapes and business requirements.

7. Regulatory Compliance:

- Stay informed about evolving regulatory requirements and ensure that cloud operations remain compliant.

8. Cybersecurity Frameworks:

- Consider adopting cybersecurity frameworks such as NIST Cybersecurity Framework or ISO 27001 to guide risk management efforts.

Conclusion:

Risk management in the cloud is a dynamic and multifaceted process that requires ongoing attention and dedication. By proactively identifying, assessing, mitigating, and monitoring risks associated with cloud adoption, organizations can minimize security threats, maintain regulatory compliance, and protect their reputation and customer trust in the ever-evolving landscape of cloud computing.

CHAPTER 10

Advanced Cloud Topics

In the ever-evolving world of cloud computing, staying ahead requires a deep understanding of not only the fundamentals but also advanced topics that are shaping the future of the cloud. This section delves into advanced cloud concepts and emerging trends that are revolutionizing the way organizations leverage cloud technology to drive innovation, scalability, and efficiency. From edge computing and quantum computing to artificial intelligence, machine learning, and blockchain integration, we embark on a journey to explore these cutting-edge topics and their implications for the cloud industry and beyond.

A. Edge Computing: Unleashing the Power of Proximity

Edge computing is a paradigm-shifting concept in the world of cloud computing that brings computation and data storage closer to the source of data generation and consumption. It addresses the limitations of traditional cloud computing, such as latency, bandwidth constraints, and privacy concerns, by enabling real-time processing and decision-making at the edge of the network. In this in-depth exploration, we delve into the significance, key components, use cases, and challenges of edge computing.

1. Significance of Edge Computing:

a. Reducing Latency:

- Edge computing significantly reduces latency by processing data closer to where it is generated. This is critical for applications requiring real-time responses, such as autonomous vehicles and industrial automation.

b. Bandwidth Optimization:

- By processing data locally, edge computing minimizes the need for sending large volumes of data to centralized cloud data centers, optimizing bandwidth usage and reducing network congestion.

c. Privacy and Security:

- Edge computing enhances data privacy and security by keeping sensitive information within a localized network, reducing exposure to external threats.

2. Key Components of Edge Computing:

a. Edge Devices:

- These include sensors, IoT devices, gateways, and edge servers that collect and preprocess data at the edge of the network.

b. Edge Computing Infrastructure:

- Edge computing infrastructure consists of edge servers, micro data centers, and edge clouds that provide computational resources for data processing and storage.

c. Edge Computing Software:

- Edge computing software platforms enable application deployment, orchestration, and management at the edge. These platforms often support containerization and orchestration tools like Kubernetes.

d. Connectivity Technologies:

- High-speed, low-latency connectivity technologies such as 5G play a crucial role in facilitating communication between edge devices and the centralized cloud.

3. Use Cases of Edge Computing:

a. Autonomous Vehicles:

- Edge computing enables real-time processing of sensor data for autonomous navigation, collision avoidance, and decision-making.

b. Industrial IoT (IIoT):

- In manufacturing and industry, edge computing supports predictive maintenance, quality control, and process optimization.

c. Smart Cities:

- Edge computing powers smart city applications like traffic management, waste management, and environmental monitoring.

d. Healthcare:

- Edge devices can process patient data locally, supporting telemedicine, remote patient monitoring, and real-time diagnostics.

e. Content Delivery:

- Edge computing improves content delivery by caching content closer to end-users, reducing latency in video streaming and content distribution.

f. Retail:

- Retailers use edge computing for inventory management, customer analytics, and personalized shopping experiences.

4. Challenges and Considerations:

a. Scalability:

- Managing a distributed edge infrastructure can be complex and requires scalable solutions.

b. Security:

- Securing edge devices and infrastructure is critical, as they are often more exposed to physical threats.

c. Standardization:

- There is a need for standardized protocols and APIs to enable interoperability among diverse edge devices and platforms.

d. Data Management:

- Managing and synchronizing data between edge and central cloud environments can be challenging.

e. Cost:

- Deploying and maintaining edge infrastructure can be cost-intensive, especially for organizations with numerous edge locations.

f. Edge-to-Cloud Integration:

- Effective integration between edge and central cloud

environments is essential to harness the full potential of edge computing.

Conclusion:

Edge computing represents a transformative shift in the cloud computing landscape, enabling real-time processing, reducing latency, and improving privacy and security. It has a profound impact on various industries, from autonomous vehicles to healthcare and manufacturing. However, implementing and managing edge computing infrastructure comes with its own set of challenges, including scalability, security, and data management. As technology continues to advance, the potential applications and benefits of edge computing are poised to grow, making it an exciting frontier in the world of cloud computing.

B. Quantum Computing and the Cloud: A New Frontier in Computational Power

Quantum computing is a groundbreaking technological advancement that leverages the principles of quantum mechanics to perform computations that were previously unimaginable with classical computers. The cloud has emerged as a vital platform for quantum computing, offering access to quantum resources, algorithms, and services that hold the promise of revolutionizing industries and solving complex problems. In this in-depth exploration, we delve into the significance, principles, applications, challenges, and future implications of quantum computing in the cloud.

1. Significance of Quantum Computing:

a. Exponential Computational Power:

- Quantum computers harness the unique properties of quantum bits or qubits, which can exist in multiple states simultaneously. This parallelism enables quantum computers to solve complex problems exponentially faster than classical computers.

b. Revolutionary Applications:

- Quantum computing has the potential to transform fields such as cryptography, drug discovery, material science, optimization, and artificial intelligence by tackling problems that were previously intractable.

2. Key Principles of Quantum Computing:

a. Superposition:

- Qubits can exist in a superposition of states, representing both 0 and 1 simultaneously. This property allows quantum computers to perform parallel computations.

b. Entanglement:

- Qubits can become entangled, meaning the state of one qubit is dependent on the state of another, even if they are physically separated. This property is fundamental for quantum communication and computing.

c. Quantum Gates:

- Quantum algorithms are constructed using quantum gates, analogous to classical logic gates but operating on qubits.

d. Quantum Algorithms:

- Quantum algorithms, such as Shor's algorithm and Grover's algorithm, exploit quantum properties to solve specific problems faster than classical algorithms.

3. Quantum Computing in the Cloud:

a. Quantum Cloud Services:

- Cloud providers like IBM, Amazon, Microsoft, and Google offer quantum cloud services, providing access to quantum computers, simulators, and development tools.

b. Quantum-as-a-Service (QaaS):

- QaaS platforms enable researchers, developers, and organizations to run quantum algorithms and experiments in the cloud without the need to invest in quantum hardware.

4. Applications of Quantum Computing:

a. Cryptography:

- Quantum computers threaten classical cryptographic algorithms like RSA and ECC, leading to the development of quantum-resistant encryption methods.

b. Drug Discovery:

- Quantum computing can simulate molecular interactions at a quantum level, accelerating drug discovery and development.

c. Optimization:

- Quantum algorithms can solve complex optimization problems in logistics, finance, and supply chain management more efficiently.

d. Artificial Intelligence:

- Quantum machine learning algorithms have the potential to enhance AI capabilities, enabling faster training and better pattern recognition.

e. Materials Science:

- Quantum computing can simulate the behavior of

materials at the atomic and molecular levels, leading to the discovery of novel materials with unique properties.

5. Challenges of Quantum Computing:

a. Hardware Development:

- Building and maintaining stable and error-resistant quantum hardware remains a significant challenge.

b. Quantum Error Correction:

- Mitigating errors caused by decoherence and noise in quantum systems is crucial for practical quantum computing.

c. Scalability:

- Scaling quantum hardware and algorithms to handle large and complex problems is a formidable task.

d. Security Concerns:

- Quantum computers pose a threat to classical encryption methods, necessitating the development of quantum-resistant cryptography.

6. Future Implications:

- Quantum computing is still in its early stages, but its potential impact on various industries is profound. The integration of quantum computing with classical cloud services will likely lead to hybrid computing models that combine the strengths of both classical and quantum computing.

Conclusion:

Quantum computing in the cloud represents a convergence of cutting-edge technologies with the potential to revolutionize industries, solve complex problems, and transform the way we approach computation. While quantum computing faces significant challenges in terms of hardware development and error correction, it holds promise for addressing critical issues in cryptography, drug discovery, materials science, and optimization. As quantum technologies mature and become more accessible through cloud services, they will likely reshape the future of computing and innovation.

C. Artificial Intelligence and Machine Learning in the Cloud: Transforming Data into Insights

Artificial intelligence (AI) and machine learning (ML) have emerged as powerful tools for extracting valuable insights, automating tasks, and making data-driven decisions. When combined with the scalability and flexibility of cloud computing, AI and ML solutions become even more accessible and capable of addressing complex challenges. In this in-depth exploration, we delve into the significance, principles, use cases, challenges, and future directions of AI and ML in the cloud.

1. Significance of AI and ML in the Cloud:

a. Scalability and Flexibility:

- Cloud computing provides the resources and infrastructure needed to scale AI and ML workloads to handle vast datasets and complex computations.

b. Accessibility:

- Cloud-based AI and ML services democratize access to advanced machine learning tools and technologies, making them available to a broader audience.

c. Cost Efficiency:

- Pay-as-you-go pricing models in the cloud enable organizations to use AI and ML resources efficiently without significant upfront investments.

d. Integration:

- Cloud platforms offer seamless integration of AI and ML services with existing applications, databases, and workflows.

2. Key Principles of AI and ML in the Cloud:

a. Data Collection and Preprocessing:

- High-quality data is the foundation of effective AI and ML models. Cloud platforms provide tools for data collection, cleaning, and transformation.

b. Model Development and Training:

- Cloud-based ML frameworks and services offer the computational power and algorithms necessary for training complex machine learning models.

c. Deployment and Inference:

- Deploy trained models as APIs or services in the cloud to make predictions and inferences on new data.

d. Automation and Optimization:

- Cloud-based ML services often incorporate automation and optimization features to streamline the ML pipeline.

3. Use Cases of AI and ML in the Cloud:

a. Predictive Analytics:

- AI and ML models in the cloud are used for predictive maintenance, demand forecasting, and fraud detection.

b. Natural Language Processing (NLP):

- Cloud-based NLP models power chatbots, sentiment analysis, and language translation services.

c. Computer Vision:

- Cloud services enable image and video analysis for tasks like object detection, facial recognition, and autonomous vehicles.

d. Recommendation Systems:

- AI-driven recommendation engines enhance user experiences in e-commerce, streaming services, and content personalization.

e. Healthcare:

- AI and ML in the cloud support medical image analysis, disease diagnosis, and drug discovery.

f. Financial Services:

- AI models are used for risk assessment, algorithmic trading, and credit scoring in the financial sector.

g. Manufacturing:

- Cloud-based AI and ML optimize production processes, quality control, and supply chain management.

4. Challenges of AI and ML in the Cloud:

a. Data Privacy and Security:

- Handling sensitive data in the cloud requires robust security measures to protect against breaches and data leaks.

b. Model Bias and Fairness:

- Ensuring AI and ML models are fair and unbiased is an ongoing challenge, requiring careful data curation and model evaluation.

c. Model Interpretability:

- Understanding and explaining the decisions made by complex AI models is a critical challenge for regulatory compliance and trust.

d. Ethical Considerations:

- AI and ML technologies in the cloud raise ethical questions related to privacy, discrimination, and transparency.

e. Skill Gap:

- The shortage of AI and ML expertise presents a challenge for organizations looking to implement these technologies effectively.

5. Future Directions:

- AI and ML in the cloud are expected to evolve with advancements in deep learning, reinforcement learning, and quantum computing.

- Federated learning and edge AI will enable more decentralized and efficient AI processing.

Conclusion:

AI and ML in the cloud represent a transformative force that is reshaping industries, enhancing decision-making, and driving innovation. The combination of scalable cloud resources and advanced AI and ML tools provides organizations with the means to tackle complex problems, improve efficiencies, and unlock new insights from their data. However, addressing challenges related to data privacy, model bias, and ethics will be crucial as AI and ML continue to play an increasingly central role in our digital world.

D. Blockchain and Cloud Integration: Harnessing the Power of Distributed Ledgers

Blockchain technology has disrupted industries by providing a secure and transparent means of recording transactions and data. When integrated with cloud computing, blockchain can offer enhanced security, reliability, and efficiency for various applications. In this in-depth exploration, we delve into the significance, principles, use cases, challenges, and future potential of integrating blockchain with cloud technology.

1. Significance of Blockchain and Cloud Integration:

a. Enhanced Security:

- Blockchain's decentralized and immutable ledger adds an extra layer of security when integrated with cloud services, reducing the risk of data manipulation and unauthorized access.

b. Transparency and Trust:

- Blockchain provides transparency by enabling all parties to verify transactions and data, fostering trust in cloud-based processes.

c. Data Integrity:

- Integrating blockchain ensures the integrity of data, making it tamper-proof and reducing the likelihood of data corruption.

2. Key Principles of Blockchain and Cloud Integration:

a. Decentralization:

- Blockchain technology relies on a network of nodes,

reducing the dependence on a single centralized entity, which aligns with the distributed nature of cloud computing.

b. Smart Contracts:

- Smart contracts are self-executing agreements with predefined rules encoded on the blockchain, automating processes and interactions within cloud-based applications.

c. Data Anchoring:

- Blockchain can be used to anchor critical data or metadata to ensure its integrity and timestamp for legal or compliance purposes.

d. Identity and Access Management:

- Blockchain can enhance identity and access management (IAM) by providing a secure and decentralized way to manage user identities.

3. Use Cases of Blockchain and Cloud Integration:

a. Supply Chain Management:

- Blockchain integrated with cloud services enhances transparency and traceability in supply chains, helping organizations monitor the movement of goods and verify authenticity.

b. Healthcare Data:

- Secure storage and sharing of patient health records on the cloud, with blockchain ensuring data integrity and patient consent.

c. Financial Services:

- Combining cloud infrastructure with blockchain enables faster and more secure cross-border payments and settlements.

d. Intellectual Property and Copyright:

- Blockchain can be used to timestamp and protect intellectual property rights by anchoring copyrights on an immutable ledger.

e. Voting Systems:

- Cloud-based voting systems can benefit from blockchain's security and transparency to prevent fraud and ensure the integrity of elections.

4. Challenges of Blockchain and Cloud Integration:

a. Scalability:

- Integrating blockchain with cloud services may face scalability issues due to the resource-intensive nature of blockchain networks.

b. Interoperability:

- Ensuring compatibility and seamless interaction between blockchain platforms and cloud services can be challenging.

c. Regulatory Compliance:

- Addressing legal and regulatory concerns, especially in highly regulated industries, is essential for successful integration.

d. Cost:

- Implementing blockchain and cloud integration can incur additional costs, including transaction fees on blockchain networks.

5. Future Potential:

- Advances in blockchain technology, such as sharding and consensus mechanisms, may alleviate scalability challenges and enhance integration capabilities.

- The convergence of blockchain, cloud, and IoT can lead to new applications in various domains, including supply chain, healthcare, and smart cities.

Conclusion:

Blockchain and cloud integration represents a convergence of two transformative technologies that can enhance security, transparency, and trust in a wide range of applications. While there are challenges to overcome, the potential benefits of this integration are substantial, particularly in industries where data integrity, traceability, and trust are paramount. As both blockchain and cloud technologies continue to evolve, their integration is likely to play a pivotal role in shaping the future of data management and secure, decentralized applications.

CHAPTER 11

Exploring Future Trends in Cloud Computing

The landscape of cloud computing is in a perpetual state of transformation, driven by rapid technological advancements and evolving business needs. As we venture into the future, it is imperative to anticipate the emerging trends that will shape the cloud industry. In this introductory overview, we embark on a journey to explore the future trends in cloud computing, encompassing topics such as edge AI and IoT, serverless computing advancements, the impact of quantum computing, ethical and sustainable cloud computing practices, and predictions that will reshape the cloud industry as we know it. These trends represent the convergence of innovation, technology, and sustainability, offering exciting possibilities for organizations worldwide.

A. Edge AI and IoT: Transforming the Future of Computing

Edge Artificial Intelligence (AI) and the Internet of Things (IoT) represent two converging technologies that are poised to revolutionize the way we process data and make intelligent decisions. Together, they bring AI capabilities closer to data sources, enabling real-time analysis, reduced latency, and improved efficiency. In this in-depth exploration, we delve into the significance, principles, use cases, challenges, and future implications of Edge AI and IoT.

1. Significance of Edge AI and IoT:

a. Real-time Decision-Making:

- Edge AI brings AI inferencing capabilities to IoT devices, allowing them to make instant decisions without relying on cloud-based processing.

b. Latency Reduction:

- By processing data locally, Edge AI reduces the latency associated with sending data to centralized cloud servers.

c. Bandwidth Efficiency:

- Edge AI filters and compresses data at the source, reducing the need for transmitting large volumes of data to the cloud, which optimizes bandwidth usage.

d. Offline Capabilities:

- Edge AI enables devices to operate autonomously even when disconnected from the cloud, enhancing their usability in remote or intermittent connectivity scenarios.

2. Key Principles of Edge AI and IoT:

a. On-device Inference:

- Edge AI devices perform inferencing tasks locally, without relying on cloud resources.

b. Data Filtering and Preprocessing:

- IoT devices preprocess data at the edge to reduce noise and transmit only relevant information to the cloud.

c. Low-power and Compact Computing:

- Edge AI devices are designed to be energy-efficient and often employ specialized hardware, such as GPUs or TPUs, for AI processing.

d. Real-time Responsiveness:

- Edge AI systems must provide real-time responses, making them suitable for applications like autonomous vehicles and robotics.

3. Use Cases of Edge AI and IoT:

a. Smart Home Automation:

- Edge AI powers intelligent home devices, from thermostats and security cameras to voice assistants, making homes more responsive and energy-efficient.

b. Industrial IoT (IIoT):

- Edge AI enhances manufacturing processes by monitoring equipment, predicting maintenance needs, and optimizing production.

c. Autonomous Vehicles:

- Edge AI enables real-time decision-making in self-driving cars, ensuring safety and responsiveness.

d. Healthcare Wearables:

- Wearable devices with Edge AI can monitor vital signs, detect anomalies, and provide timely alerts to healthcare providers.

e. Retail Inventory Management:

- Edge AI systems help retailers optimize inventory, reduce theft, and enhance the shopping experience.

f. Agriculture:

- IoT sensors equipped with Edge AI can monitor soil conditions, crop health, and livestock, enabling precision agriculture.

4. Challenges of Edge AI and IoT:

a. Resource Constraints:

- Edge devices have limited processing power and memory, which can limit the complexity of AI models that can run locally.

b. Data Security:

- Protecting data on Edge AI devices from physical and cyber threats is crucial.

c. Scalability:

- Managing a large number of Edge AI devices across various locations can be challenging.

d. Model Updates:

- Keeping AI models on Edge devices up to date with the latest improvements and security patches requires a reliable mechanism.

5. Future Implications:

- Edge AI and IoT are likely to continue evolving with advancements in AI hardware, federated learning, and 5G connectivity.

- New applications may emerge as Edge AI and IoT

become more deeply integrated into various industries.

Conclusion:

Edge AI and IoT are ushering in a new era of computing, where intelligence is distributed across a vast array of devices. The ability to make real-time decisions locally, reduce latency, and enhance data security is transforming industries ranging from healthcare and manufacturing to transportation and agriculture. While challenges exist, the future of Edge AI and IoT holds promise for innovative applications and improved efficiency, making it an exciting frontier in the world of technology and data processing.

B. Serverless Computing Advancements: Shaping the Future of Cloud-Native Development

Serverless computing has emerged as a transformative paradigm in cloud computing, allowing developers to focus on code without the burden of managing servers or infrastructure. Over the years, serverless technologies have evolved, offering more capabilities, flexibility, and scalability. In this in-depth exploration, we delve into the significance, principles, advancements, use cases, and future trends in serverless computing.

1. Significance of Serverless Computing:

a. Simplified Development:

- Serverless allows developers to focus solely on writing code, eliminating the need to manage servers, scaling, or infrastructure provisioning.

b. Cost Efficiency:

- With serverless, you only pay for the resources your code consumes when it runs, reducing costs compared to traditional server-based approaches.

c. Scalability and Elasticity:

- Serverless platforms automatically scale to handle varying workloads, ensuring applications remain responsive even during traffic spikes.

2. Key Principles of Serverless Computing:

a. Event-Driven Architecture:

- Serverless functions are triggered by events, such as HTTP requests, database changes, or scheduled tasks.

b. Stateless Functions:

- Serverless functions are stateless, meaning they do not store data between invocations. They rely on external data stores or services.

c. Pay-as-You-Go Pricing:

- Serverless platforms charge based on the number of function invocations and the time they execute, ensuring cost efficiency.

d. Microservices Integration:

- Serverless functions can be used as microservices, enabling modular and scalable application architectures.

3. Advancements in Serverless Computing:

a. Multi-Language Support:

- Serverless platforms have expanded language support, allowing developers to use their preferred programming languages.

b. Improved Cold Start Times:

- Efforts to reduce cold start times have made serverless functions more responsive and suitable for a broader range of use cases.

c. Stateful Workloads:

- Some serverless platforms now support stateful workloads, enabling more complex applications.

d. Serverless Containers:

- Container-based serverless offerings provide more control and flexibility for deploying serverless functions.

4. Use Cases of Serverless Computing:

a. Web Applications:

- Serverless is ideal for web applications, handling functions like authentication, data processing, and content delivery.

b. Real-time Data Processing:

- Serverless can process real-time data streams from IoT devices, social media, or sensors.

c. Batch Processing:

- Serverless functions can perform batch processing tasks, such as data transformation or image processing.

d. APIs and Microservices:

- Serverless is well-suited for building APIs and microservices to support scalable and modular architectures.

e. Chatbots and Voice Assistants:

- Serverless functions power chatbots and voice

assistants, handling natural language processing and interaction logic.

5. Future Trends in Serverless Computing:

a. Improved Cold Start Performance:

- Ongoing efforts will likely further reduce cold start times, making serverless more suitable for latency-sensitive applications.

b. Edge Computing Integration:

- Combining serverless with edge computing will enable low-latency processing at the edge of the network.

c. Hybrid Cloud Deployments:

- Serverless platforms may offer hybrid cloud capabilities, allowing organizations to run functions in both public and private clouds.

d. Enhanced Observability:

- Improved tools for monitoring and debugging serverless applications will simplify troubleshooting and performance optimization.

Conclusion:

Serverless computing has come a long way since its inception, offering a simplified and cost-effective approach to cloud-native development. With advancements in language support, cold start times, and stateful workloads, serverless computing is well-positioned to play a pivotal role in modern application development. As it continues to evolve, we can expect even greater adoption across various industries and innovative use cases, reshaping the way we build and deploy cloud-native applications.

C. Quantum Computing Impact: Unlocking the Potential of Unconventional Computing

Quantum computing represents a revolutionary shift in the world of computing, offering the promise of solving complex problems at speeds unimaginable with classical computers. Its impact on various fields, from cryptography to drug discovery, is profound and continues to grow. In this in-depth exploration, we delve into the significance, principles, applications, challenges, and future implications of quantum computing.

1. Significance of Quantum Computing:

a. Exponential Speedup:

- Quantum computers leverage the principles of quantum mechanics, allowing them to solve certain problems exponentially faster than classical computers.

b. Game-Changing Applications:

- Quantum computing has the potential to transform fields such as cryptography, materials science, optimization, and machine learning.

c. Security and Cryptography:

- Quantum computers pose a threat to classical encryption methods, spurring the development of quantum-resistant encryption.

d. Drug Discovery and Materials Science:

- Quantum computing accelerates molecular simulations, leading to the discovery of new drugs and materials.

2. Key Principles of Quantum Computing:

a. Qubits:

- Quantum bits or qubits can exist in multiple states simultaneously, enabling quantum computers to process vast amounts of information in parallel.

b. Superposition:

- Qubits can exist in a superposition of states, representing both 0 and 1 at the same time, allowing for parallel computations.

c. Entanglement:

- Qubits can become entangled, meaning the state of one qubit is dependent on the state of another, even if they are physically separated. This property is fundamental for quantum communication and computing.

d. Quantum Gates:

- Quantum algorithms are constructed using quantum gates, analogous to classical logic gates but operating on qubits.

3. Applications of Quantum Computing:

a. Cryptography:

- Quantum computers threaten classical cryptographic algorithms like RSA and ECC, leading to the development of quantum-resistant encryption methods.

b. Drug Discovery:

- Quantum computing can simulate molecular interactions at the quantum level, accelerating drug discovery and development.

c. Optimization:

- Quantum algorithms can solve complex optimization problems in logistics, finance, and supply chain management more efficiently.

d. Artificial Intelligence:

- Quantum machine learning algorithms have the potential to enhance AI capabilities, enabling faster training and better pattern recognition.

e. Materials Science:

- Quantum computing can simulate the behavior of materials at the atomic and molecular levels, leading to the discovery of novel materials with unique properties.

4. Challenges of Quantum Computing:

a. Hardware Development:

- Building and maintaining stable and error-resistant quantum hardware remains a significant challenge.

b. Quantum Error Correction:

- Mitigating errors caused by decoherence and noise in quantum systems is crucial for practical quantum computing.

c. Scalability:

- Scaling quantum hardware and algorithms to handle large and complex problems is a formidable task.

d. Security Concerns:

- Quantum computers pose a threat to classical encryption methods, necessitating the development of quantum-resistant cryptography.

5. Future Implications:

- Quantum computing is still in its early stages, but its potential applications and benefits are poised to grow as technology continues to advance.

- Quantum technologies may also lead to new paradigms in communication, sensing, and materials science.

Conclusion:

Quantum computing represents a disruptive force in the world of computing and science. Its impact is already visible in fields such as cryptography and materials science, and as quantum technologies mature, their applications are likely to expand into diverse domains. Overcoming challenges related to hardware, error correction, and scalability is crucial for unlocking the full potential of quantum computing, which has the power to reshape industries and drive innovation in ways we can only begin to imagine.

D. Ethical and Sustainable Cloud Computing: Navigating the Digital Frontier Responsibly

As cloud computing continues to permeate nearly every aspect of our digital lives, ethical and sustainable considerations have become increasingly significant. Ensuring that cloud technologies are used responsibly and with minimal environmental impact is a pressing concern. In this in-depth exploration, we delve into the significance, principles, challenges, and future implications of ethical and sustainable cloud computing.

1. Significance of Ethical and Sustainable Cloud Computing:

a. Environmental Impact:

- Data centers that power cloud services consume vast amounts of energy and have a significant carbon footprint. Addressing sustainability is essential to mitigate environmental harm.

b. Privacy and Security:

- Ethical cloud computing entails safeguarding user data and maintaining privacy while preventing unauthorized access and data breaches.

c. Responsible AI and Automation:

- Ethical considerations are paramount when developing

AI algorithms and automation systems to ensure fairness, transparency, and accountability.

d. Compliance and Regulation:

- Cloud providers must adhere to regional and international regulations, such as GDPR, HIPAA, and environmental standards, to maintain ethical and sustainable practices.

2. Principles of Ethical and Sustainable Cloud Computing:

a. Energy Efficiency:

- Data centers should employ energy-efficient technologies, such as renewable energy sources, and minimize wastage to reduce their carbon footprint.

b. Data Privacy and Security:

- Cloud providers must implement robust security measures, encryption, and access controls to protect user data.

c. Transparency and Accountability:

- Transparency in data handling, AI decision-making, and accountability for any breaches or errors are essential ethical principles.

d. Fair AI and Automation:

- AI algorithms should be trained and tested for fairness, avoiding biases and discrimination.

e. Responsible Sourcing:

- Ethical cloud providers should source hardware and materials responsibly, avoiding conflict minerals and unethical practices.

3. Challenges in Ethical and Sustainable Cloud Computing:

a. Energy Consumption:

- Data centers require massive amounts of energy, and many are powered by non-renewable sources, contributing to environmental concerns.

b. Data Privacy and Security:

- Ensuring data privacy while maintaining security against cyber threats is a delicate balance.

c. Ethical AI:

- Developing AI systems that are fair, unbiased, and transparent remains a complex challenge.

d. Compliance and Regulation:

- Adhering to evolving regulations across different regions and industries can be challenging for cloud providers.

e. E-Waste Management:

- Disposal and recycling of electronic waste (e-waste) from decommissioned hardware pose environmental concerns.

4. Future Implications:

a. Green Cloud Computing:

- Sustainable practices, such as using renewable energy, cooling optimization, and data center location planning, will be crucial for reducing the environmental impact of cloud computing.

b. Ethical AI and Transparency:

- Advancements in AI ethics will lead to more transparent and accountable AI systems.

c. Regulatory Frameworks:

- The development of standardized global regulations for data privacy, security, and environmental responsibility will shape the future of ethical cloud computing.

d. Consumer Awareness:

- Increased awareness among consumers and businesses about ethical and sustainable cloud practices will drive demand for responsible cloud providers.

Conclusion:

Ethical and sustainable cloud computing is a multifaceted challenge that encompasses environmental responsibility, data privacy, security, fairness in AI, and adherence to regulations. As cloud technology continues to evolve, the principles of ethics and sustainability will play an increasingly significant role in shaping the industry. Cloud providers, businesses, and consumers must collectively work toward responsible cloud practices to harness the benefits of digital transformation while minimizing its negative consequences on the environment and society.

E. Predictions for the Cloud Industry: Shaping the Digital Frontier

The cloud industry is in a perpetual state of evolution, driven by technological advancements, changing business needs, and emerging trends. Predicting the future of cloud computing is an exercise in anticipating how these factors will shape the industry. In this in-depth exploration, we delve into some key predictions for the cloud industry, shedding light on the potential developments that may redefine the way we use and perceive cloud technology.

1. Multi-Cloud Adoption Will Become the Norm:

As organizations seek to diversify their cloud strategies and mitigate vendor lock-in risks, multi-cloud adoption will continue to rise. Companies will leverage multiple cloud providers to achieve flexibility, redundancy, and optimization for their workloads.

2. Edge Computing Will Gain Momentum:

Edge computing, which brings computational power closer to data sources and users, will see substantial growth. Edge environments will become essential for latency-sensitive applications, such as IoT, augmented reality, and real-time analytics.

3. Cloud-Native Technologies Will Proliferate:

The adoption of cloud-native technologies, such as containers and microservices, will continue to expand. These technologies enable organizations to build and scale applications more efficiently and are central to modern application development.

4. Quantum Computing Will Impact Cloud Services:

Quantum computing will move from experimental phases to

practical applications within the cloud industry. Quantum cloud services may become available, opening up new possibilities in cryptography, optimization, and scientific research.

5. AI and Machine Learning Integration Will Deepen:

AI and machine learning will become more deeply integrated into cloud platforms, offering advanced analytics, automation, and intelligent insights. Cloud-based AI services will enable businesses to harness the power of machine learning with ease.

6. Security and Compliance Will Be Paramount:

Security and compliance concerns will remain at the forefront of cloud adoption. Cloud providers will continue to invest in advanced security measures, and regulatory compliance will drive industry standards.

7. Serverless Computing Will Continue to Evolve:

Serverless computing will evolve with improvements in cold start times, language support, and stateful capabilities. More organizations will embrace serverless architectures for event-driven applications.

8. Cloud Skills Gap Will Persist:

The shortage of cloud expertise will continue, emphasizing the importance of cloud training and certifications. Cloud providers and educational institutions will collaborate to address the skills gap.

9. Sustainable Cloud Practices Will Gain Traction:

Sustainability will become a significant focus in the cloud industry. Cloud providers will invest in renewable energy sources, efficient data center designs, and eco-friendly practices to reduce their carbon footprint.

10. Hybrid and Multi-Cloud Management Tools Will Thrive:

The demand for tools and platforms that simplify the management of hybrid and multi-cloud environments will grow. Businesses will seek solutions that provide unified visibility and control over their cloud resources.

11. 5G and Cloud Synergy Will Drive Innovation:

The synergy between 5G networks and cloud computing will lead to innovative applications in IoT, edge computing, augmented reality, and remote collaboration.

12. Ethical AI and Responsible Cloud Practices Will Prevail:

The ethical use of AI and responsible cloud practices will become a competitive advantage. Businesses will prioritize fairness, transparency, and accountability in their AI and cloud initiatives.

Conclusion:

The cloud industry's future is marked by dynamic and transformative changes. As technology continues to advance, the cloud will remain a critical enabler of digital transformation, driving innovation, efficiency, and competitiveness across industries. While these predictions provide a glimpse into what lies ahead, the cloud's true potential may well exceed our expectations, shaping the digital landscape in ways we can only imagine. Businesses and IT professionals will need to adapt and evolve alongside these trends to harness the full benefits of cloud technology.

CHAPTER 12

Case Studies and Use Cases

In the ever-evolving world of cloud computing, real-world examples of successful cloud adoption serve as beacons of inspiration and guidance. In this section, we delve into case studies and use cases that illuminate the practical applications, challenges, and triumphs of cloud technology across various industries. These stories offer invaluable insights and lessons learned, providing a roadmap for businesses and professionals seeking to navigate their own cloud journeys.

A. Real-world examples of successful cloud adoption: Lessons from Industry Pioneers

Successful cloud adoption is not merely a theoretical concept but a tangible achievement for organizations across diverse sectors. In this exploration, we delve into real-world examples of companies that have harnessed the power of cloud computing to transform their operations, achieve scalability, and drive innovation. These case studies offer valuable insights into the strategies, challenges, and outcomes of successful cloud adoption.

1. Netflix:

- **Challenge:** At the peak of its DVD rental business, Netflix faced the challenge of transitioning to a streaming service while accommodating rapid growth and fluctuating demand.
- **Cloud Solution:** Netflix embraced Amazon Web Services (AWS) to host its streaming platform. This allowed them to scale resources on-demand, optimize content delivery through CDNs, and improve viewer experiences.
- **Outcome:** Netflix's cloud adoption enabled it to become a global streaming giant with millions of subscribers worldwide. The flexibility and scalability of AWS played a pivotal role in this transformation.

2. Airbnb:

- **Challenge:** Airbnb needed a scalable and cost-effective infrastructure to handle the rapid growth of its online marketplace for lodging and travel experiences.
- **Cloud Solution:** Airbnb migrated its entire platform to AWS, leveraging services like Amazon EC2, Amazon RDS, and Amazon S3 for hosting, database management, and data storage.
- **Outcome:** By adopting the cloud, Airbnb reduced infrastructure costs, improved reliability, and achieved global

scalability. The move allowed the company to expand rapidly, becoming a household name in the sharing economy.

3. Slack:

- **Challenge:** Slack aimed to create a collaborative messaging platform that could support millions of users and integrate seamlessly with other business tools.

- **Cloud Solution:** Slack chose to build its platform on top of AWS, utilizing AWS Lambda for serverless computing and Amazon S3 for data storage.

- **Outcome:** Slack's cloud-native architecture enabled it to rapidly scale its user base and integrate with a wide range of third-party applications. The company became a leader in team collaboration software.

4. NASA's Mars Rover Missions:

- **Challenge:** NASA needed to collect, process, and transmit massive volumes of data from Mars rovers while dealing with unpredictable mission requirements.

- **Cloud Solution:** NASA's Jet Propulsion Laboratory (JPL) utilized AWS for the Mars Rover missions. They employed AWS Lambda, Amazon S3, and EC2 for data processing, storage, and computational tasks.

- **Outcome:** AWS's cloud capabilities allowed NASA to manage the complexity of Mars missions efficiently. It facilitated data analysis, mission planning, and real-time monitoring, contributing to the success of rover missions like Curiosity and Perseverance.

5. GE Healthcare:

- **Challenge:** GE Healthcare sought to provide scalable and secure cloud solutions for its healthcare clients while maintaining regulatory compliance.

- **Cloud Solution:** GE Healthcare partnered with Microsoft Azure to develop the Edison platform, which offers secure, AI-powered healthcare applications and services on the cloud.

- **Outcome:** Edison has enabled GE Healthcare to deliver innovative healthcare solutions, including medical image analysis and patient data management, while ensuring compliance with stringent healthcare regulations.

Conclusion:

These real-world case studies illustrate the transformative power of cloud adoption. Whether it's streaming media, sharing economy platforms, collaboration tools, space exploration, or healthcare, the cloud has become an indispensable enabler of growth, scalability, and innovation. These success stories underscore the importance of strategic planning, cloud provider partnerships, and the ability to adapt to changing technology landscapes in achieving successful cloud adoption.

B. Industry-specific use cases: Tailoring Cloud Solutions for Success

Cloud computing is not a one-size-fits-all solution. Its adaptability allows it to be tailored to meet the unique needs of various industries. In this exploration, we delve into industry-specific use cases that showcase how organizations leverage cloud technology to address specific challenges, enhance operations, and drive innovation across diverse sectors.

1. Healthcare:

Use Case: Telemedicine and Remote Patient Monitoring

- **Challenge:** The healthcare industry required a solution to improve access to medical services, reduce costs, and enable remote patient monitoring.
- **Cloud Solution:** Cloud-based telemedicine platforms enable patients to consult with healthcare providers via video calls. IoT devices collect and transmit patient data to the cloud for real-time monitoring.
- **Outcome:** Patients can access healthcare services from

anywhere, reducing the need for in-person visits. Continuous monitoring helps in early detection and intervention, improving patient outcomes.

2. Financial Services:

Use Case: Risk Analysis and Fraud Detection

- **Challenge:** Financial institutions face the constant threat of fraud and must assess risk accurately to make informed lending decisions.
- **Cloud Solution:** Cloud-based analytics platforms analyze vast datasets to detect anomalies and patterns indicative of fraud. Machine learning models provide real-time risk assessments.
- **Outcome:** Financial organizations can identify fraudulent activities swiftly and enhance risk management, reducing financial losses and protecting customer assets.

3. Retail:

Use Case: E-commerce Scalability

- **Challenge:** Retailers must handle surges in online shopping during peak seasons while maintaining a seamless customer experience.
- **Cloud Solution:** Retailers utilize cloud-based e-commerce

platforms that auto-scale to handle increased traffic. Cloud storage manages product catalogs, images, and customer data.

- **Outcome:** Retailers can manage peak demand efficiently, ensuring website stability and timely order processing, while also optimizing costs during slower periods.

4. Manufacturing:

Use Case: Supply Chain Optimization

- **Challenge:** Manufacturers require real-time visibility into their supply chains to minimize disruptions and optimize inventory.
- **Cloud Solution:** Cloud-based supply chain management systems integrate data from suppliers, logistics providers, and production facilities. Advanced analytics provide insights for demand forecasting and inventory management.
- **Outcome:** Manufacturers can streamline operations, reduce costs, and improve supply chain resilience, ensuring timely production and delivery of goods.

5. Education:

Use Case: Remote Learning

- **Challenge:** Educational institutions needed a solution to deliver online education effectively, especially during the

COVID-19 pandemic.

- **Cloud Solution:** Cloud-based learning management systems (LMS) facilitate remote teaching and learning. These platforms offer video conferencing, content sharing, and assessment tools.

- **Outcome:** Educational institutions can continue teaching and engage students remotely, ensuring continuity of education during disruptions.

6. Energy:

Use Case: Smart Grids and Energy Management

- **Challenge:** The energy sector sought ways to enhance grid reliability, optimize energy distribution, and promote sustainability.

- **Cloud Solution:** Cloud-based smart grid solutions leverage IoT sensors to collect data on energy usage and grid conditions. Advanced analytics and machine learning enable real-time energy management.

- **Outcome:** Utilities can reduce energy waste, respond to outages faster, and integrate renewable energy sources into the grid efficiently.

7. Entertainment and Media:

Use Case: Content Streaming and Personalization

- **Challenge:** The media industry needed to provide on-demand content to a global audience while delivering personalized recommendations.
- **Cloud Solution:** Cloud-based content delivery networks (CDNs) ensure fast and reliable streaming. Machine learning algorithms analyze user behavior to recommend content.
- **Outcome:** Media companies can reach a global audience with high-quality streaming and engage viewers with personalized content recommendations.

Conclusion:

These industry-specific use cases illustrate the versatility and adaptability of cloud computing. By tailoring cloud solutions to address their unique challenges and objectives, organizations in various sectors can unlock new opportunities for growth, efficiency, and innovation. Cloud technology continues to play a pivotal role in transforming industries and driving digital evolution.

C. Lessons Learned and Best Practices in Cloud Computing

Cloud computing has revolutionized the way businesses operate, offering scalability, agility, and cost-efficiency. However, navigating the cloud landscape isn't without challenges. In this exploration, we delve into the lessons learned and best practices that organizations have gleaned from their cloud journeys, helping others make the most of this transformative technology.

1. Plan and Strategize:

- **Lesson Learned:** Rushing into the cloud without a clear strategy can lead to inefficiencies, increased costs, and security risks.
- **Best Practice:** Begin with a well-defined cloud strategy that aligns with your business objectives. Conduct a thorough assessment of your current infrastructure and identify workloads suitable for migration.

2. Security is Paramount:

- **Lesson Learned:** Neglecting security measures can result in data breaches and financial losses.
- **Best Practice:** Implement robust security practices, including encryption, access controls, and regular security audits.

Leverage cloud provider security tools and stay informed about emerging threats.

3. Cost Management:

- **Lesson Learned:** Underestimating cloud costs can lead to budget overruns.
- **Best Practice:** Use cloud cost monitoring tools to track spending and optimize resources. Implement cost-saving strategies such as auto-scaling, reserved instances, and rightsizing.

4. Backup and Disaster Recovery:

- **Lesson Learned:** Data loss or downtime can have severe consequences if not adequately prepared for.
- **Best Practice:** Implement a robust backup and disaster recovery (DR) plan. Leverage cloud-based DR solutions for data redundancy and failover capabilities.

5. Compliance and Governance:

- **Lesson Learned:** Neglecting compliance requirements can lead to legal and regulatory issues.
- **Best Practice:** Understand the compliance requirements specific to your industry and region. Implement governance frameworks and audit trails to demonstrate compliance to

regulators.

6. Training and Skill Development:

- **Lesson Learned:** A lack of cloud expertise can hinder successful adoption.
- **Best Practice:** Invest in cloud training and certifications for your IT team. Encourage continuous learning to keep up with evolving cloud technologies.

7. Vendor Lock-In Mitigation:

- **Lesson Learned:** Over-reliance on a single cloud provider can limit flexibility.
- **Best Practice:** Adopt multi-cloud or hybrid cloud strategies to reduce vendor lock-in. Use cloud-agnostic tools and design applications for portability.

8. Monitoring and Performance Optimization:

- **Lesson Learned:** Neglecting performance monitoring can lead to inefficiencies and degraded user experiences.
- **Best Practice:** Implement robust monitoring and performance optimization practices. Utilize cloud provider monitoring tools and automate scaling based on performance metrics.

9. Data Management:

- **Lesson Learned:** Poor data management can result in data silos and reduced insights.
- **Best Practice:** Establish data governance policies, including data classification and access controls. Leverage cloud data analytics services for actionable insights.

10. Collaboration and Communication:

- **Lesson Learned:** Effective collaboration and communication are essential for cloud success.
- **Best Practice:** Foster collaboration between IT, development, and business teams. Use cloud-based collaboration tools and ensure clear communication channels.

11. Scalability and Flexibility:

- **Lesson Learned:** Failing to adapt to changing needs can hinder business growth.
- **Best Practice:** Design applications for scalability and elasticity. Leverage cloud services that allow you to scale resources up or down as needed.

12. Ethical and Sustainable Practices:

- **Lesson Learned:** Ignoring ethical and sustainability

considerations can damage reputation and hinder long-term success.

- **Best Practice:** Integrate ethical principles and sustainability into your cloud strategy. Seek eco-friendly cloud providers and promote responsible AI practices.

Conclusion:

The lessons learned and best practices highlighted here provide a roadmap for organizations embarking on their cloud computing journeys. By prioritizing security, cost management, compliance, and skill development while fostering collaboration and scalability, businesses can harness the full potential of the cloud while avoiding common pitfalls. As cloud technology continues to evolve, embracing these lessons and practices will be essential for maintaining a competitive edge and achieving long-term success.

Conclusion

As we draw the final curtain on this journey through these pages, we invite you to reflect on the knowledge, insights, and discoveries that have unfolded before you. Our exploration of various subjects has been a captivating voyage into the depths of understanding.

In these chapters, we have ventured through the intricacies of numerous topics and examined the key concepts and findings that define these fields. It is our hope that you have found inspiration, enlightenment, and valuable takeaways that resonate with you on your own quest for knowledge.

Remember that the pursuit of understanding is an ever-evolving journey, and this book is but a milestone along the way. The world of knowledge is vast and boundless, offering endless opportunities for exploration and growth.

As you conclude this book, we encourage you to carry forward the torch of curiosity and continue your exploration of these subjects. Seek out new perspectives, engage in meaningful discussions, and embrace the thrill of lifelong learning.

We express our sincere gratitude for joining us on this intellectual adventure. Your curiosity and dedication to expanding your horizons are the driving forces behind our shared quest for wisdom and insight.

Thank you for entrusting us with a portion of your intellectual journey. May your pursuit of knowledge lead you to new heights and inspire others to embark on their own quests for understanding.

With sincere appreciation,

Nikhilesh Mishra, Author

Recap of Key Takeaways

As we conclude our exploration of "**Mastering Cloud Computing: Concepts, Techniques, and Applications**" let's revisit and summarize the key takeaways from this comprehensive guide. These essential insights encapsulate the knowledge you've gained about cloud computing and its multifaceted aspects:

1. Cloud Computing Fundamentals:

- **Definition and Evolution:** Cloud computing has evolved into a transformative technology that provides on-demand access to shared computing resources via the internet, revolutionizing IT infrastructure.

- **Key Concepts:** Understanding virtualization, scalability, and elasticity is crucial as these concepts underpin cloud computing's efficiency and adaptability.

- **Service Models:** Cloud service models—Infrastructure as a Service (IaaS), Platform as a Service (PaaS), and Software as a Service (SaaS)—offer varying levels of abstraction and management responsibilities.

- **Deployment Models:** Public, private, hybrid, and multi-cloud deployment models cater to diverse business needs, providing flexibility, control, and scalability.

2. Cloud Infrastructure:

- **Data Centers and Server Farms:** Cloud providers operate extensive data centers and server farms worldwide, serving as the foundation for cloud services.
- **Virtualization Technologies:** Virtualization optimizes resource utilization by enabling multiple virtual machines (VMs) to run on a single physical server.
- **Storage Systems:** Different types of cloud storage, including block, object, and file storage, accommodate various data storage requirements.
- **Networking in the Cloud:** Cloud networking technologies facilitate secure, scalable, and high-performance communication between cloud resources and users.

- **Cloud Hardware and Software:** Cloud providers develop specialized hardware and software components to meet cloud-specific demands, such as load balancing, redundancy, and automation.

3. Cloud Service Providers:

- **Leading Cloud Providers:** Recognizable names like AWS, Azure, and Google Cloud offer extensive services and global infrastructure, enabling businesses to scale and innovate.

- **Regional and Niche Providers:** Regional and specialized cloud providers cater to specific markets and may offer advantages like data sovereignty or industry expertise.

- **Comparison of Services:** Evaluating cloud providers involves assessing factors like service offerings, pricing models, and global reach to select the most suitable provider.

- **Vendor Lock-In and Portability:** Consider strategies for maintaining flexibility and data portability to mitigate potential vendor lock-in.

4. Cloud Security:

- **Cloud Security Models:** Shared responsibility models outline security responsibilities for cloud providers and users, emphasizing collaborative efforts to secure cloud resources.
- **Identity and Access Management:** Effective identity management and access controls are paramount for safeguarding data and resources in the cloud.
- **Data Encryption and Compliance:** Data encryption, both in transit and at rest, ensures data confidentiality, while compliance measures address regulatory requirements.
- **Security Best Practices:** Implement best practices, such as least privilege access, regular patching, and security monitoring, to enhance cloud security.
- **Incident Response and Recovery:** Develop comprehensive incident response and recovery plans to mitigate the impact of security breaches and data loss.

5. Cloud Networking:

- **Virtual Private Cloud (VPC):** VPCs create isolated network environments within the cloud, enhancing security and network segmentation.

- **Content Delivery Networks (CDNs):** CDNs improve content delivery by caching data at edge locations, reducing latency and enhancing user experiences.

- **Cloud Networking Protocols:** Familiarize yourself with protocols like HTTP, HTTPS, and BGP used for efficient communication and routing in the cloud.

- **Hybrid and Multi-Cloud Networking:** Networking solutions facilitate seamless communication between on-premises infrastructure, multiple cloud providers, and services.

- **Performance Optimization:** Implement performance optimization strategies, such as content compression and load balancing, to enhance application responsiveness.

6. Cloud Computing Architectures:

- **Microservices and Serverless Computing:** These architectural patterns enable agile development, scalability, and efficient resource utilization.

- **Containers and Orchestration (Kubernetes):** Containers and container orchestration platforms like Kubernetes simplify application deployment and management.

- **DevOps and CI/CD:** DevOps practices, combined with continuous integration and continuous deployment (CI/CD) pipelines, streamline application development and delivery.

- **Cloud-Native Applications:** Building cloud-native applications leverages cloud services and architecture, enhancing scalability and resilience.

7. Cloud Storage and Databases:

- **Cloud Storage Services:** Choose the appropriate cloud storage services, such as Amazon S3 or Azure Blob Storage, based on your data storage needs.

- **NoSQL and SQL Databases in the Cloud:** NoSQL and SQL databases offer diverse data storage options for various application requirements.

- **Data Warehousing and Analytics:** Cloud-based data warehousing and analytics solutions enable organizations to harness the power of big data.

- **Data Migration and Backup Strategies:** Develop strategies for migrating data to the cloud and implementing robust backup and recovery plans.

8. Cloud Cost Management:

- **Cost Structures in the Cloud:** Understand cloud cost structures, including pay-as-you-go, reserved instances, and spot instances.

- **Cost Monitoring and Optimization Tools:** Leverage cost monitoring and optimization tools to track spending and identify areas for cost reduction.

- **Budgeting and Forecasting:** Establish budgeting and

forecasting practices to effectively manage cloud expenses and align them with organizational goals.

- **Strategies for Cost Reduction:** Implement strategies such as resource rightsizing, automation, and spot instance usage to reduce cloud costs while maintaining performance.

These key takeaways encompass the essential knowledge and skills you've acquired on your journey through cloud computing. They serve as a solid foundation for successfully navigating the complex and ever-evolving world of cloud technology. Remember that cloud computing is a dynamic field, and staying informed and adaptable is essential for continued success and innovation.

The Future of Cloud Computing

As we gaze into the future of cloud computing, we see a landscape marked by transformative technologies, innovative strategies, and an evolving ecosystem. Cloud computing has become an integral part of the digital revolution, and its trajectory promises to reshape industries, economies, and the way we live and work. Here are some key trends and predictions that offer insights into the future of cloud computing:

1. Edge Computing Dominance:

- *Edge AI and IoT*: Edge computing, coupled with artificial intelligence (AI) and the Internet of Things (IoT), will gain prominence. Processing data closer to its source will reduce latency and enable real-time decision-making in critical applications, from autonomous vehicles to smart cities.

- *5G Integration*: The rollout of 5G networks will accelerate edge computing adoption, enabling faster data transmission and supporting a multitude of low-latency, high-bandwidth applications.

2. Serverless Computing Advancements:

- *FaaS Growth*: Serverless computing, or Function as a Service (FaaS), will continue to grow, simplifying development and scaling of applications. More languages, runtimes, and event-driven services will be supported.

- *Multi-Cloud Serverless*: Multi-cloud support for serverless functions will become common, allowing organizations to leverage the best features of different cloud providers without lock-in.

3. Quantum Computing Impact:

- *Quantum Cloud Services*: Quantum computing will enter the cloud, offering quantum processing as a service. This will accelerate research, cryptography, and optimization in various fields.

- *Security and Cryptography*: Quantum computing will also challenge existing encryption methods, spurring the development of quantum-resistant cryptographic techniques.

4. Ethical and Sustainable Cloud Computing:

- *Ethical AI*: The ethical implications of AI and cloud computing will be a major focus. Companies will adopt ethical AI principles and practices, addressing bias, fairness, and transparency.

- *Sustainability*: Sustainability will become a core concern. Cloud providers will increasingly use renewable energy, and sustainable cloud practices will gain prominence.

5. Evolving Cloud-Native Architectures:

- *Serverless Containers*: The convergence of serverless and container technologies will lead to serverless containers, combining the benefits of both.

- *Cloud-Native Security*: Security will be deeply integrated into cloud-native architectures, emphasizing proactive threat detection and response.

6. Industry-Specific Cloud Solutions:

- *Healthcare and Life Sciences*: Cloud solutions tailored to healthcare and life sciences will accelerate research, drug discovery, and personalized medicine.

- *Financial Services*: The financial industry will adopt cloud-based analytics, fraud detection, and blockchain solutions, while ensuring regulatory compliance.

7. Hybrid and Multi-Cloud Expansion:

- *Interoperability*: Seamless interoperability between different cloud providers will be a priority, enabling organizations to distribute workloads optimally.

- *Hybrid Cloud Growth*: Hybrid cloud adoption will grow, driven by the need for data privacy, compliance, and disaster recovery solutions.

8. Continued Innovation and Competition:

- *Innovation Hubs*: Leading cloud providers will establish innovation hubs and research centers to drive technological advancements and stay competitive.

- *Startup Ecosystem*: Cloud services will continue to empower startups, enabling them to scale rapidly and innovate without heavy infrastructure investment.

9. Ethical and Legal Frameworks:

- *Data Privacy*: Stricter data privacy regulations will emerge globally, influencing how data is stored and processed in the cloud.
- *Digital Sovereignty*: Countries may assert digital sovereignty, leading to localized cloud ecosystems and data residency requirements.

10. Skills and Talent Development:

- *Cloud Skills Gap*: The demand for cloud-related skills will surge, necessitating continuous learning and upskilling for IT professionals.
- *Cloud Certifications*: Industry-recognized cloud certifications will play a crucial role in validating expertise.

11. AI-Driven Automation:

- *Automated Cloud Management*: AI-driven tools will automate cloud management tasks, optimizing resource allocation and cost management.

- *Predictive Analytics*: Predictive analytics will be used to anticipate cloud resource needs and potential issues.

12. Quantum-Enhanced AI:

- *Quantum Machine Learning*: Quantum computing will intersect with AI, leading to advancements in quantum-enhanced machine learning and optimization.

13. Regulatory Compliance:

- *GDPR-like Regulations*: More regions and countries will implement GDPR-like regulations, placing stricter requirements on cloud providers and users.

14. Resilience and Disaster Recovery:

- *Resilience Planning*: Organizations will prioritize cloud-based disaster recovery and resilience planning to ensure business continuity.

15. Cloud Cost Management:

- *Advanced Cost Analytics*: Advanced cost analytics and optimization tools will help organizations manage cloud spending efficiently.

The future of cloud computing promises a world of possibilities, from faster and smarter applications to ethical AI and sustainable practices. As cloud technology evolves, businesses and individuals must adapt, embracing innovation while addressing emerging challenges. Staying informed, continuously learning, and being agile will be essential for thriving in the ever-expanding universe of cloud computing.

Glossary of Terms

Navigating the world of cloud computing involves understanding a multitude of technical terms and concepts. In this glossary, we'll explore key terms and their meanings to help you build a comprehensive understanding of cloud computing:

1. Cloud Computing:

- Definition: Cloud computing refers to the delivery of computing services (e.g., storage, processing, networking) over the internet, providing on-demand access to resources and services without the need for on-premises infrastructure.

2. Virtualization:

- Definition: Virtualization is the technology that allows multiple virtual instances (e.g., virtual machines or containers) to run on a single physical server, improving resource utilization and isolation.

3. Scalability:

- Definition: Scalability refers to the ability to efficiently increase or decrease computing resources as needed, ensuring that applications can handle varying workloads without disruption.

4. Elasticity:

- Definition: Elasticity is a subset of scalability that focuses on the automatic allocation and deallocation of resources based on real-time demand, optimizing resource utilization and cost efficiency.

5. Infrastructure as a Service (IaaS):

- Definition: IaaS is a cloud service model that provides virtualized computing resources over the internet, including virtual machines, storage, and networking.

6. Platform as a Service (PaaS):

- Definition: PaaS is a cloud service model that offers a platform for developers to build, deploy, and manage applications without worrying about underlying infrastructure.

7. Software as a Service (SaaS):

- Definition: SaaS is a cloud service model that delivers software applications over the internet on a subscription basis, eliminating the need for local installation and maintenance.

8. Public Cloud:

- Definition: A public cloud is a cloud computing environment hosted by a third-party provider, offering resources to the general public over the internet.

9. Private Cloud:

- Definition: A private cloud is a cloud computing environment exclusively dedicated to a single organization, providing greater control and security.

10. Hybrid Cloud:

Definition: A hybrid cloud combines both public and private cloud resources, allowing data and applications to move seamlessly between them.

11. Multi-Cloud:

Definition: Multi-cloud refers to the use of multiple cloud providers to avoid vendor lock-in, enhance redundancy, and optimize services based on specific provider strengths.

12. Vendor Lock-In:

Definition: Vendor lock-in occurs when an organization becomes dependent on a specific cloud provider's services, making it challenging to migrate to an alternative provider.

13. Data Center:

Definition: A data center is a facility that houses servers, storage systems, and networking equipment, providing the physical infrastructure for cloud computing services.

14. Virtual Private Cloud (VPC):

Definition: A VPC is a logically isolated section of a public cloud's network where an organization can launch resources with defined network configurations.

15. Content Delivery Network (CDN):

Definition: A CDN is a network of distributed servers strategically placed to deliver web content, such as images and videos, to users with reduced latency and improved performance.

16. Load Balancing:

Definition: Load balancing is the process of distributing incoming network traffic across multiple servers to ensure even resource utilization and high availability.

17. Redundancy:

Definition: Redundancy involves duplicating critical components or data to ensure system availability and fault tolerance in case of hardware or software failures.

18. High Availability (HA):

Definition: High availability refers to the ability of a system or application to remain operational and accessible with minimal downtime.

19. DevOps:

Definition: DevOps is a set of practices that combine development (Dev) and IT operations (Ops) to automate and streamline the software development and deployment process.

20. Continuous Integration/Continuous Deployment (CI/CD):

Definition: CI/CD is a set of practices that automate code integration, testing, and deployment, enabling rapid and reliable software delivery.

21. Microservices:

Definition: Microservices is an architectural approach where applications are broken down into small, independent services that can be developed and deployed separately.

22. Containers:

Definition: Containers are lightweight, portable, and self-contained environments that package applications and their dependencies, ensuring consistency across different environments.

23. Kubernetes:

Definition: Kubernetes is an open-source container orchestration platform that automates the deployment, scaling, and management of containerized applications.

24. Data Warehousing:

Definition: Data warehousing is the process of collecting, storing, and managing large volumes of structured data for analytics and reporting purposes.

25. Compliance:

Definition: Compliance refers to adherence to legal and regulatory requirements, such as GDPR or HIPAA, to protect data privacy and security in the cloud.

26. Encryption:

Definition: Encryption is the process of converting data into a secure format to prevent unauthorized access, ensuring data confidentiality.

27. Data Migration:

Definition: Data migration involves moving data from one location or format to another, often from on-premises environments to the cloud.

28. Cost Optimization:

Definition: Cost optimization in the cloud involves managing and reducing cloud expenses through efficient resource allocation, monitoring, and cost analysis.

29. Governance:

Definition: Governance in cloud computing involves establishing policies, procedures, and controls to manage and monitor cloud resources, ensuring compliance and security.

30. Quantum Computing:

Definition: Quantum computing is a cutting-edge field that leverages the principles of quantum mechanics to perform complex computations at speeds unattainable by classical computers.

This glossary provides a foundation for understanding the terminology and concepts that shape the world of cloud computing. As the cloud continues to evolve, staying familiar with these terms will empower you to make informed decisions and navigate the cloud landscape effectively.

Resources and References

As you reach the final pages of this book by Nikhilesh Mishra, consider it not an ending but a stepping stone. The pursuit of knowledge is an unending journey, and the world of information is boundless.

Discover a World Beyond These Pages

We extend a warm invitation to explore a realm of boundless learning and discovery through our dedicated online platform: **www.nikhileshmishra.com**. Here, you will unearth a carefully curated trove of resources and references to empower your quest for wisdom.

Unleash the Potential of Your Mind

- **Digital Libraries:** Immerse yourself in vast digital libraries, granting access to books, research papers, and academic treasures.

- **Interactive Courses:** Engage with interactive courses and lectures from world-renowned institutions, nurturing your thirst for knowledge.

- **Enlightening Talks:** Be captivated by enlightening talks delivered by visionaries and experts from diverse fields.

- **Community Connections:** Connect with a global community of like-minded seekers, engage in meaningful discussions, and share your knowledge journey.

Your Journey Has Just Begun

Your journey as a seeker of knowledge need not end here. Our website awaits your exploration, offering a gateway to an infinite universe of insights and references tailored to ignite your intellectual curiosity.

Acknowledgments

As I stand at this pivotal juncture, reflecting upon the completion of this monumental work, I am overwhelmed with profound gratitude for the exceptional individuals who have been instrumental in shaping this remarkable journey.

In Loving Memory

To my father, **Late Shri Krishna Gopal Mishra,** whose legacy of wisdom and strength continues to illuminate my path, even in his physical absence, I offer my deepest respect and heartfelt appreciation.

The Pillars of Support

My mother**, Mrs. Vijay Kanti Mishra,** embodies unwavering resilience and grace. Your steadfast support and unwavering faith in my pursuits have been the bedrock of my journey.

To my beloved wife, **Mrs. Anshika Mishra,** your unshakable belief in my abilities has been an eternal wellspring of motivation. Your constant encouragement has propelled me to reach new heights.

My daughter, **Miss Aarvi Mishra,** infuses my life with boundless joy and unbridled inspiration. Your insatiable curiosity serves as a constant reminder of the limitless power of exploration and discovery.

Brothers in Arms

To my younger brothers, **Mr. Ashutosh Mishra** and **Mr. Devashish Mishra,** who have steadfastly stood by my side, offering unwavering support and shared experiences that underscore the strength of familial bonds.

A Journey Shared

This book is a testament to the countless hours of dedication and effort that have gone into its creation. I am immensely grateful for the privilege of sharing my knowledge and insights with a global audience.

Readers, My Companions

To all the readers who embark on this intellectual journey alongside me, your curiosity and unquenchable thirst for knowledge inspire me to continually push the boundaries of understanding in the realm of cloud computing.

With profound appreciation and sincere gratitude,

Nikhilesh Mishra

September 17, 2023

About the Author

Nikhilesh Mishra is an extraordinary visionary, propelled by an insatiable curiosity and an unyielding passion for innovation. With a relentless commitment to exploring the boundaries of knowledge and technology, Nikhilesh has embarked on an exceptional journey to unravel the intricate complexities of our world.

Hailing from the vibrant and diverse landscape of India, Nikhilesh's pursuit of knowledge has driven him to plunge deep into the world of discovery and understanding from a remarkably young age. His unwavering determination and quest for innovation have not only cemented his position as a thought leader but have also earned him global recognition in the ever-evolving realm of technology and human understanding.

Over the years, Nikhilesh has not only mastered the art of translating complex concepts into accessible insights but has also crafted a unique talent for inspiring others to explore the limitless possibilities of human potential.

Nikhilesh's journey transcends the mere boundaries of expertise; it is a transformative odyssey that challenges conventional wisdom and redefines the essence of exploration. His commitment to pushing the boundaries and reimagining the norm serves as a luminous beacon of inspiration to all those who aspire to make a profound impact in the world of knowledge.

As you navigate the intricate corridors of human understanding and innovation, you will not only gain insight into Nikhilesh's expertise but also experience his unwavering dedication to empowering readers like you. Prepare to be enthralled as he seamlessly melds intricate insights with real-world applications, igniting the flames of curiosity and innovation within each reader.

Nikhilesh Mishra's work extends beyond the realm of authorship; it is a reflection of his steadfast commitment to shaping the future of knowledge and exploration. It is an embodiment of his boundless dedication to disseminating wisdom for the betterment of individuals worldwide.

Prepare to be inspired, enlightened, and empowered as you embark on this transformative journey alongside Nikhilesh Mishra. Your understanding of the world will be forever enriched, and your passion for exploration and innovation will reach new heights under his expert guidance.

Sincerely, **A Fellow Explorer**

Notes

Notes

Notes

Notes

Notes

Notes

www.ingramcontent.com/pod-product-compliance
Lightning Source LLC
LaVergne TN
LVHW051433050326
832903LV00030BD/3067

* 9 7 9 8 8 6 1 6 5 3 1 6 9 *